W9-ACE-392

CHILDREN'S GAMES
THROUGHOUT THE YEAR

1 THE CRICKETER, *c.* 1850

Frontispiece

From a watercolour by W. Hunt (1790–1864)

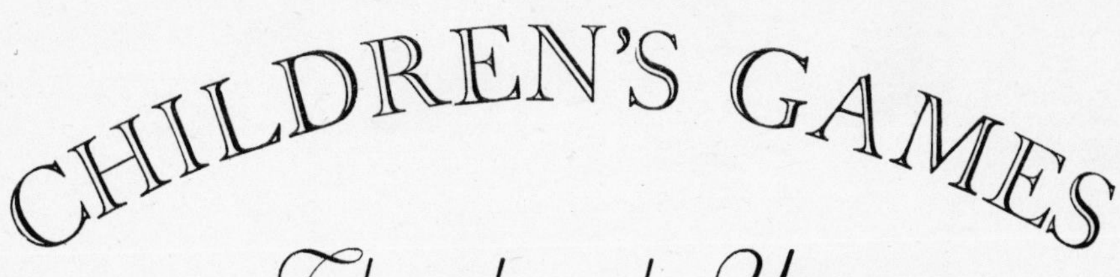

CHILDREN'S GAMES

Throughout the Year

By

Leslie Daiken

B. T. BATSFORD LTD.
LONDON · NEW YORK · TORONTO · SYDNEY

First published, Autumn, 1949

TO MY TWO DAUGHTERS
AND TO ALL THE WORLD'S CHILDREN
I DEDICATE THIS BOOK

. . . or little children playing with bare feet
Upon the sands of some ebbed shore
In Connaught; things young and happy . . .

And then my heart hath told me, "These will pass,
Will pass and fade, will die and be no more";
And I have gone upon my way, sorrowful.

PADRAIC PEARSE

MADE AND PRINTED IN GREAT BRITAIN
BY JARROLD AND SONS LTD., NORWICH FOR THE PUBLISHERS B. T. BATSFORD LTD.,
LONDON: 15 NORTH AUDLEY STREET, W.1 AND MALVERN WELLS, WORCESTERSHIRE
NEW YORK: 122 EAST 55TH STREET TORONTO: 480–6 UNIVERSITY AVENUE
SYDNEY: 156 CASTLEREAGH STREET

ACKNOWLEDGMENTS

Boys and Girls Come Out To Play
The Moon doth shine as bright as day.
Come with a whoop, come with a call,
Come with a goodwill or don't come at all;
Lose your supper and lose your sleep,
So come to your playmates in the street.

THE DANCING MASTER, 1728

It is a pleasure for me to acknowledge the help which I have received from all those whose writings and sympathetic interest have lit up my years of labour, so often interrupted. I must refer with gratitude especially to the two volumes which Lady Alice B. Gomme prepared for the British Folklore Society, and which were published in 1898—before my time—as the *Dictionary of British Folklore;* this work afforded me the first signposts towards Irish fields of research, and urged me along trackways and bohareens to seek new evidence; and to the following who have generously given me permission to use quotations, drawings and photographs:

Messrs. Macmillan & Co., for two drawings by Hugh Thomson, pp. 41 and 53, from *Highways and Byways in London*, and for excerpts from *I Knock at the Door* by Sean O'Casey; Messrs. Frederick Warne & Co., for the Kate Greenaway subjects used for the dust-jacket and Fig. 54; and for several drawings from *Games and Sports for Young Boys* (1862); Messrs. Faber and Faber, for excerpts from *Country Things* by Alison Uttley; Messrs. Gollancz, for excerpts from *Play in Childhood* by Margaret Lowenfeld; Messrs. David Nutt, for excerpts and the drawings on pp. 72, 73, 75, 143, 199, from *Traditional Games of England, Scotland and Ireland* by Alice B. Gomme; Messrs. Marcus Ward & Co., for drawings by T. Pym on title page, pp. 16, 119, 195, and Figs. 50, 55 and 105, from *Skipping Time* (1867); Messrs. George Routledge & Sons, for drawings on pp. 74, 112, 174, 200 and Figs. 75, 76, from *Summer Songs of Country Life* (1865); Messrs. George Bell & Sons Ltd., for drawing on p. 142 from Gomme's *Parlour and Playground Games*; Messrs. Sampson Low, for Figs. 59, 60 from *Child's Play* (1866), given to me by Miss I. Wright; Messrs. Novello & Co., for musical excerpts from *Singing Games*, edited by Cecil Sharp; *Country Life*, for Fig. 88; *Illustrated London News*, for Figs. 107, 108; Dansk Folkemindesamling, København, for drawing on pp. vi, 4 and 146 and Figs. 51, 71; the

Trustees of the British Museum, for engravings on pp. 123, 124, from Didereichs: *Deutsches Leben*, vol. II (1618); prints from the Canon Collection, Figs. 39, 68; prints by Francis Hayman, Figs. 4, 38, 42, 101; numerous illustrations by the Brothers Dalziel; and Figs. 2, 3, 10, 49, 108, 110; the Librarian, Bodleian Library, Oxford, for drawings on pp. 27, 57, 127, 167, 170, and Figs. 5, 9, 15, 16, 18, 20, 21, 26, 27, 28, 29, 30, 31, 33, 34, 35, 41, 52, 58, 62, 65, 79, 81, 82, 84, 85, 87, 90, 91, 92, 93, 94, 95, 98, 99, 100, 102, 103, 113, 114, from the Douce Folios; Messrs. W. F. Mansell, for Fig. 71; Messrs. W. T. Spencer's collection, for Figs. 13, 14, 69, 70, 106, 107; the Court Bookshop, London, for Figs. 24, 43, 57, 63, 64; Mr. R. Weaver Smith, for Figs. 89, 109 and drawing on p. 178; Mr. Colm O'Lochlainn for woodcut on p. 212; Mr. George Gilmore, for linocut on p. 59; Dr. G. Gemmill, for Fig. 56; and my warmest thanks also to the following for suggestions, encouragement and co-operation while this work was being written: Mr. Alec Rowley who edited the musical score; Mr. Sean O'Sullivan, Archivist at the Irish Folklore Commission; Rev. Eric Mac Fhinn of Galway; the Hon. Mrs. J. ffrench of Castle-ffrench; Mr. Hugh Quinn of Belfast; Dr. James Starkey and Professor W. B. Stanford, of Dublin; Mr. Simon Campbell, Mrs. Bernadette Easton and Mr. Robert Farren (for rhymes); Mr. S. Gibson, formerly sub-Librarian at the Bodleian Library, Oxford; Mr. Snelgrove (Prints and Engravings Department) and Mr. Skeat (Manuscripts Department) of the British Museum; Messrs. A. L. Norrington and Charles Batey of the Oxford University Press; Mr. D. Billington of Messrs. Frederick Warne & Co.; Mr. John Larmour, Mr. A. Bassous, Mr. J. O'Rorke, Headmaster of St. Patrick's (L.C.C.) School; Mr. Thomas Fassam, Mr. R. Vreeland and Miss Watkins of Messrs. W. T. Spencer, for valued help. I am happy to add the name of my publishers, including Brian C. Batsford, for directing the design and layout of this book.

LESLIE DAIKEN

MIDDLESEX
September 1949

CONTENTS

From an old Aramaic Singing Game

"They are like unto children who frequent the market-place,
And who call out, some unto others, and say:

WE PIPED UNTO YOU WITH PIPES
AND YOU DANCED NOT;
WE WAILED UNTO YOU A LAMENT
AND YOU WEPT NOT."

(St. Luke vii. 32)

דּוֹמִים הֵם לַיְלָדִים הַיֹּשְׁבִים בַּשּׁוּק וְקֹרְאִים זֶה אֶל־זֶה
וְאֹמְרִים

הִלַּלְנוּ לָכֶם בַּחֲלִילִים | וְלֹא רְקַדְתֶּם ‖
קוֹנַנּוּ לָכֶם קִינָה | וְלֹא בְכִיתֶם ‖

January

This month calls for games that keep you warm; games of running about and rough-and-tumbles.

If snow falls—Tobogganing, Snowballing and Skating (2), naturally enough, become the order of the day; while Making

Snowmen is mid-winter's especial rite (3). The month has a martial urge and favours, therefore, the PURSUIT GAME, the COMBAT GAME, GAMES OF CAPTURE.

TOUCH

Any number of boys can play at this popular game. One of the players volunteers to be *Touch* or *He*, or else he is chosen to fill that office by counting out (see "Rhymes and Calls"[1]). *Touch* then endeavours, by following after, to touch one of his playmates as they run about in all directions trying to avoid him. When a player is touched he becomes *Touch*, and in his turn strives to touch one of the others. When *Touch* succeeds in touching another, he cries "Feign double-touch!", which signifies that the player so touched must not touch the player who touched him, until he has chased somebody else.

TOUCH-WOOD AND TOUCH-IRON

These games are founded on the above. When the boys pursued by *Touch* can touch either wood or iron they are safe, the rule being that he must touch them as they run from one piece of wood or iron to another.

FOUR RHYMES FOR TIG

I

One-ery, two-ery, ziccary zeven;
Hollow bone, crack a bone, ten or eleven;
Spin, spon, it must be done;
Twiddledum, twaddledum, twenty-one.
O-U-T, spells out,
A nasty dirty dish-clout;
Out boys out!

II

Een-a, deen-a, dine-a, dust,
Cat'll-a, ween-a, wine-a, wust,
Spin, spon, must be done,
Twiddlum, twaddlum, twenty-one,
O-U-T, spells out,
A nasty dirty dish-clout;
Out boys out!

III

Hickety, pickety, pize-a-rickety,
Pompalorum jig;
Make a posset of good ale,
And I will have a swig.
O-U-T, spells out,
A hole in a shoe, and never a clout,
Out boys out!

IV

Eena meena macker racker
Rare, ro, domino,
Juliacker, alapacker,
Rom, Tom, tush!

Pursuit Games originate in the ancient tribal custom of the Hunt, which they dramatise. The usual pattern of all these games involves (*a*) two sections, pursuers and pursued; (*b*) a

[1] Space restrictions leave no room for an appendix containing the text of forty Tig Rhymes which I have collected.

region agreed by everybody as being "safe"; and (*c*) the bringing home of captive or quarry as the consummation of the chase.

Horace mentions just such a game as having been popular among Roman children, similar to *Officers and Commanders*. Another reference occurs in *The Epistles*, presumably a variety of *Prisoner's Base*, which Horace alludes to in this way:

> *At pueri ludentes "rex eris" aiunt*
> *"si recte facies"; (Hic mures ahensis esto,*
> *nil conscibere sibi*),[1]

and by way of commentary, E. S. Shuckburgh tells us that "these lines refer to some game of skill where the best boy is called King". Orelli quotes Suetonius, Ner 35 *ducatus et imperia ludere*, "to play a game of Officers and Commanders".

Another commentator on the classics, Dr. A. A. Watkins, explains that "the full trochaic tetrameter is: '*Rex eris, si recte facies, si non facies non eris*'", meaning, "if you play well we will make you our king", while Connington gives an English rendering as "Deal fairly, youngster, and we'll crown you King".

Finally, in his *Ars Poetica*, Horace makes use of the phrase "*Occupet extremum scabies . . .*", meaning, "May the plague take the last player", or, as we might say nowadays, "Devil take the hindmost".

The association of this Latin catch-phrase with metal, and its obvious connection with the mythology of *Tig*, has prompted several scholars of the classics to deal with what is called "The Magic Potency of Metal" theory. A fascinating literature exists around it, and, to mention a recent contribution only, *Walls of Brass in Literature*, by Dr. E. W. Wormell,[2] offers an exhaustive examination.

In ancient Greece, Kathleen Freeman tells us,[3] they had a game by the name of *Copperfly*. It resembled, I imagine, *Blind Man's Buff*, which is a derivation of the Pursuit Game. Another favourite evidently was the *Potsherd Game*, Ostrakinda,[4] in which two teams of players lined up in front of their respective "dens" and were committed to advance or retreat in response to the Greek words for "Day" and "Night", shouted by a leader. The

[1] *The Epistles*, I, lines 59 and 60.
[2] *Hermathæna*, 1941–2.
[3] *Greece and Rome*, vol. IV, Blind Man's Buff.
[4] Ibid., No. 16, 1936.

modern parallel for this, most likely, would be *Rats and Rabbits*, which certainly keeps the players mentally, as well as literally, on their toes.

In Ireland tradition has a robust preference for all manner of Pursuit Games. Scarcely a town or village will you find where

varying forms of *Fox and Geese*, *Hare and Hounds*, *Spy for Riders*, *Hunt the Fox*, *Relivio* and *Cockalerum*, are not generally known and liked.

Gomme records a game of the *Hide and Spy* variety played in Cork "quite parallel to the game of Cook, from the cry 'coo' shouted out by the players when they have hidden themselves". Indeed, the reverberate shrill music of this human siren-note can be heard (to this day) echoing through gardens and woods and shrubberies or any suitable lie of land where excited trailers dash hotfoot towards the caller as towards faery music. A County Wexford folklorist relatively unknown to antiquarians, Kennedy by name, gives a masterly description of a Hedge School, that feature of nineteenth-century "education" in his native land. In an essay printed in *The Dublin University Magazine* for 1862[1] he remarks on the lighter side, as well as the serious side, of the curriculum: ". . . 'Prison Bars' (Prisoner's Base) was, and probably is still, the most popular of juvenile country sports; but seeing that as played by the rustics, it differed in no essential

[1] Vol. LX, p. 609, "An Irish Hedge School".

respect from the same game in vogue elsewhere, we need not particularise its rules and excellences.

Hunt the Fox often led both fox and hounds to the top of Cnoc-na Cro; but neither this game nor marbles nor peg-top requires extended notice."

In West Cork to this day they glory in *Spy for Riders*, and this is a variant, accompanied oddly enough, by a Counting-out Rhyme that I found in Skibbereen.

Players go ahide, except one. This one searches for the others; if he thinks he sees one he calls out "I see John!", etc. If he is correct, John must give him a ride on his back. If he calls out the wrong name HE must give the hiding child a ride on HIS back instead. If he calls the right name, that player must "spy" for the next round. The first spy is picked thus: they form a ring with the leader in the middle. The leader shouts:

Haina, daina, diena, duss
Cattila weela wila wuss
Hot pan Mister Dan
Tittlesome, tattlesome, number wan,
One, two, three, OUT you go.

The player on whom the word "go" falls is the person picked.

(Bfeidir gur drabuigeal Gaedilge an da line tosrig:
Lan a teidean i ndoimne dos
Cat (ag) lige a mhaoil i bfeigil abius.)[1]

[1] Verbatim, Michael O'Cullinane (schoolmaster), Skibbereen, June 1941.

The conception of immunity from attack represented by the "Base" or the area of demarcation (e.g. "home", "den", etc.) brings us to a consideration of by far the most popular, and, from investigations made, certainly the most widespread, Pursuit Game played by both boys and girls of nearly all ages: namely, the game of *Tig*.

This game combines in its play pattern three important aspects:

it includes the incantation of a rhyme before it begins, namely, the Counting-out Formula; it offers the joy of the chase, together with the thrill and skill of evasion; it evokes a subconscious sense of battling against some supernatural power, magically referred to as *It* or *He*, or the runner who "has" the onus. Concerning the rapid change and interchange of emotions experienced by children while playing *Touch*, Lowenfeld[1] observes:

> Consider, for example, the child playing *Touch*. At one moment he is part of a group being chased—he feels himself a quarry chased by a hunter, and has all the emotions of the quarry. Then comes a sudden touch. He is caught, and, after a momentary feeling of being captive, he becomes in his turn the hunter, with permission to enjoy the excitement of the chase. To play the game well and to enjoy the play the child must rejoice in this change of emotions. Indeed, the swiftly changing emotional attitudes which are characteristic of children have often bewildered adult observers.

[1] *Play in Childhood*, p. 241.

Gomme gives an account of *Cross Tig* as a game played centuries ago:[1]

> One of the players is appointed Tig. He calls out the name of the one he intends to chase and runs out after him. Another player runs across between Tig and the fugitive and then Tig runs after this cross player until another player runs between Tig and the fugitive, and so on.

There is a Dublin variant called *Tip and Tig*, a sort of mixture of *Tig* with *Tip and Run*. The game is similarly prevalent in Scotland though differently denominated. It is known as *Canlie* in Aberdeenshire and as *Tick* in Mearns: whereas in Lanarkshire and Renfrewshire it is called *Tig*. Gomme mentions a variant[2] as having been reported by one of her observers from Cork; it is there known as *Blind Man's Tig*:

> A long rope is tied to a gate or pole and one of the players holds the end of the rope, and tries to catch another player. When he succeeds in doing so, the one captured joins him (by holding hands), and helps to catch the other players. The game is finished when all are caught.

When no rope is used, but a chain of human beings all holding hands and pursuing and annexing the others, the game is also found in the form known as *Chain*; likewise as *Stag*.

In a Gaelic magazine[3] an interesting reference occurs to the word "Tig", occurring in a table of "Some Irish and other words of doubtful origin in use in the province of Leinster among English speakers." Here it is defined etymologically as: "*Come:* the well-known children's game found in Dublin." (The author's suggestion of localisation reflects a mind not wholly conversant with the facts concerning this simple game, because even if it were not played under this name in Gaelic-speaking areas, it most certainly was *not* confined to the children of Dublin!) This Irish etymological bearing on "Come" raises interesting evidence and appears to have escaped the notice of Bett, who lost the opportunity of following up this clue when he confined himself to a discussion of the word "Tag" in comparing foreign varieties

[1] *Traditional Games of England, Scotland and Ireland*, vol. I, p. 83.
[2] Ibid., p. 34.
[3] *Irisleabhar na Gaedhilige*, vol. XII (1902), p. 141.

of this game. Writes Bett:[1] "Now the game of Tag, which has developed many forms, was originally a game in which the pursued party was chased by a witch or a fairy, and saved himself from capture by *touching iron*." He further quotes from Newell[2] to show that the game was once universal in the United States, as also from Brand.[3] Nobody has considered the possible link with "Tig" (Irish for "Home") and its suggestion of "Base" or immunity.

In his *Games: Their History and Origins*, Bett notes that in Italy the game occurs as *Toccaferro* (Touch-iron), and in Germany and Switzerland called *Eisen Anfassen*, or *Eisenzech*, or *Eisenziggi*, thus strengthening his arguments that the idea behind the game goes back to an age when iron, or metal (notably bronze or brass), was held to have the power to save the pursued from his pursuer.

Despite the many interesting theories as to the philological ancestry of the word "Tig", whether it derives from *Toccaferro* or *Eisenziggi*, a more likely explanation is here advanced. The theory is based on the argument that "Tig" is a contraction from "Tigi", in which form it occurs in parts of England, e.g. "Tiggi", or as in its German equivalent "Ziggi".

If we accept this as being likely, then it is safe to argue that the word "Tig" is derived from the termination of the perfect tense of the Latin verb, *tango* = I touch, and has survived in this form to this day: *Tango*, *tangere*, *tetigi*, *tactum*. "Tetigi" evidently became shortened into "Tigi", and has its analogous meanings in both the English variant "Touch" and the Italian equivalent "Tocca"—as well as in the German parallel "Ziggi".

The conception that the pursuer may have been diabolical, or identified with the principle of Evil, is further evidenced from the fact that in parts of England (e.g. Lincolnshire) this game is known as *Horny*, and the Counting-out Rhyme used there is:

Auld Horny the Devil, burns . . .

Gomme says: "All uncouth, unknown wights are terrified by nothing earthly—so much as cold iron. . . ."

[1] *Nursery Rhymes and Tales*, p. 41.
[2] *Games and Songs of American Children*, p. 158.
[3] *Popular Antiquities*, vol. II, p. 263.

A German Counting-out Rhyme preserves this superstition:

Dreimal eiserne Stangen	*Three times iron rods*
Wer nicht läuft wird gefangen	*Who does not run will be caught*
Dreimal eiserne Schnitz	*Three times iron staves*
Wer nicht läuft wird gesitzt	*Who does not run will be made to sit;*
Dreimal über den Rhein,	*Three times over the Rhine,*
Wer nicht läuft ist mein.	*Who doesn't run is mine.*

TIG RHYMES

The most significant feature of the above rhyme is perhaps the formula of numbering. The ritual of counting out the chosen hunter from among the group, the incantation of a magical formula, based on an esoteric system of words, postulated by such a remarkable observer as Hugh Carrington Bolton,[1] were really the survivals of a primitive numeration, now become merely shreds of onamatopoeic doggerel of the "Eena-Meena-Mina-Mo" class.

Working during the end of the nineteenth century, Bolton, like Gomme, had his time cut out pioneering fields closer to his own theories, so that it can hardly have been expected of him to devote special interest to Irish material as such. Kennedy, a solitary Irish folklorist, was perhaps the only one contemporaneous with Gomme and Bolton. These English specialists, from no sense of superiority, treated Ireland as a kind of regional appendage, from which one could rely upon occasional, but always original, data cropping up. Studied analytical research on a national basis was not even considered. Yet it is of some moment that Bolton (the authority in this sphere) had, by 1888, examined 877 Counting-out Rhymes collected from widespread students, representing twenty different languages and dialects. Of the seven variants reported from Ireland, and included in his analysis, only three of them are indigenous; not one of these is from the Gaelic, an omission that seriously restricted his linguistic investigations. The Slav nations are also omitted, though Finland is represented, as are versions of Counting-out formulæ in Romany, Basque and Platt-Deutsch.

Nevertheless, we must regard Bolton as being the sole authority on the Counting-out Rhyme. It is, therefore, apposite

[1] *Counting-out Rhymes and Jingles*, 1888.

to quote in full a cross-section from the hundreds of variants that he gives in his book—the seven contributions which were reported during the middle of the last century from Ireland, and accordingly included in his anthology.

Prior to 1888:

Group III, No. 477:

One-ery, two-ery, dickery, davy,
Hallabone, crackabone, tenery, navy.
Linkum, tinkum, merrycum can,
Halibo, crackery, twenty-one.[1]

No. 505, from Limerick:

Eena, deena, dina, dass,
Bottle a weena, wina, wass;
Pin, pan, muska dan,
Eedleum, deedleum, twenty-one!
Eeery, ory, OUT goes she![2]

Group VII, No. 602:

Eena, deena, dina, doe,
Catch a nigger by the toe.
If he screams let him go,
Eena deena dina doe.[3]

Miscellaneous:

Group XI, No. 727:

My father had a fine fat pig
Now I'll give you a touch of—Tig!

No. 756:

Hiddlety, diddlety, dumpty,
The oat ran up the plum-tree,
Send a hack to fetch her back,
Iddlety, diddlety, dumpty.

No. 799:

Mitty Matty had a hen
She lays white eggs for gentlemen,
Gentlemen come every day
Mitty Matty runs away.
Hi, ho! Who is at home
Father, Mother, Jumping Joan.
O-U-T, out,
Take off the latch and walk out.[4]

No. 826:

A, B, C.
Catch the cat by the knee:
L, M, N, O,
Let the poor thing go.[5]

Now, it will be observed from these examples that, as a result of corruption and deformation, there is no specifically basic feature common to them. Imagery is, for the most part, confined to the vocabulary of the nursery, e.g. cat, pig, hen, toe, plum-tree, etc. It is only to be expected that Tig Rhymes improvised in country districts will derive their imagery from the farm-yard or the countryside, just as Tig Rhymes among city children become coloured by the vernacular of the street-characters, the

[1] Given as found in *M.H. Magazine*, vol. 127. (An analogous rhyme suggests it should end in "twenty-nine".)

[2] As sung today: "Sam, Dan, Master John", July 1941.

[3] Restricted to Irish source.

[4] Obviously a variant of "Hiddledy Piddledy".

[5] Mullingar, W. Meath.

current slang or local politics. We shall observe from a recent collection which follows,[1] just how varied the jingles may be. But they may all be grouped under one of these three headings: (*a*) Jingles based on nonsense sounds; (*b*) Jingles based on coherent rhymed narrative; (*c*) Jingles based on numeration, the alphabet, or the asking of some question involving the spelling of a word. Group (*c*) has a particular appeal, since it is the element of predestination attached to the falling of the word "Out" upon one of the players which is evocative of magic.

It is a peculiarity of some Tig Rhymes that they ramble from an initial theme to one completely outside its scope, a feature which has already been shown to be common to Skipping Rhymes. This "fusion" is not limited to rhymes in the English language, but occurs to an equal degree in Gaelic, French, Italian and other languages. Here, for instance, is a traditional Counting-out Rhyme from Florence:[2]

Cavalluccio, gio, gio, gio	*Gee up, gee up, little horsie*
piglia la biada ch'io ti do,	*Take the oats that I give you*
piglia i ferri ch'io ti metto	*Take the shoes I put on you*
per andare a San Francesco	*To go to Saint Francis*
San Francesco è buona via	*Saint Francis is well on the road*
per andare a casa mia	*To come to visit me*
a casa mia c'era un frate	*At my house there was a friar*
Che cuoceva le frittate	*Who cooked the fritters*
Me ne dette un picciolino . . .	*He gave me a little bit . . .*
Sutta via questo bambino!	*OUT goes this child!*

TOM TIDDLER'S GROUND

This is a very favourite game with young boys and may be considered as a modification of the above. A large base is formed by drawing a line across the playground, and one boy called

[1] See footnote, p. 2. [2] Elizabetta Oddone, *Cantilene Popolari dei Bimbi d'Italia* 1920.

"Tom Tiddler" takes his station within it, while the others run in, crying out "Here am I on Tom Tiddler's ground, picking up gold and silver". If Tom Tiddler can touch any boy while he is on his ground, the boy so touched takes his place as the guardian of the imaginary gold and silver.

KING OF THE CASTLE

The King of the Castle repeats the following couplet while repulsing the besiegers:

I'm the King of the Castle—
Get down you dirty rascal!

A Scottish Version:

Willie Willie Wastell	*Like Willie, Willie Wastel,*
I am on your Castle	*I am in my castle*
A' the dogs in the toon	*A' the dogs in the toun*
Winna pu Willie doon.	*Dare not ding me doun.*

The opening reference to the Roman game "rex eris" brings us to consider a similar game of Pursuit and Conquest also widely played in ancient Rome, namely, *King of the Castle*. Gomme gives a short history of the game in which she mentions a rhyme connected with it as reported from Ireland.

There exists no authoritative opinion as to the origin of the game, but the suggestion made by Dr. James Starkey seems to be the most tenable, that is, that pastoral communities have to do so much with the habits of sheep that the peculiar movements of these are among the first impressions gained by children. Children watch the young ewe-lambs frisking round a hillock, which one of their number defends most determinedly, and, as is consistent with the faculty of mimesis already discussed, they

would naturally attempt to make a game out of this amusing animal contest for supremacy. The hypothesis is strengthened by one of the *Rondes enfantines* included in Lambert's collection.[1] It is a Provençal ronde, from Lozère, recorded by M. le pasteur Liebich, Saint-Germain de Calbeste: and what more pastoral community can one find than those of Provençe?

No. V, Provençal	No. V, French:
Las fedetos e losis agnelous (*bis*)	*Les petites brebis et les agneaux*
Dansavou sus l'erbeto,	*Danseraient sur l'herbe menue,*
Las fedetos e lous agnelous	*Les petites brebis et les agneaux*
Toutes dous.	*Toutes ensemble.*

A specifically Irish variant of *King of the Castle* is the game called *Head of the Stack*. It is common to all Gaelic-speaking centres, or was, before anglicisation curtailed its spread. It was formerly played as a Game of Conquest, with a youngster defending a haycock in a field, but has since become an indoor game played with the mounting-up of fists, to the name of *Ceann an Staca*. A description appears in the periodical *Locrann*:[2]

[1] *Chants et chansons Populaires du Languedoc.* [2] January 1917, p. 4, col. 3.

They all put their fists on top of one another and the topmost one is asked a question.

Q. Cé tá ináirde?

A. Ceann an Staca.

Then they say to him:

Laig ar lár é
ar maidean amáireach
go n-íosaidh se práta
beirtite bearta
Anios C'gort a gearta
Is braoinín . . .

He then takes his fist and the same follows to the others until they reach the last person. He then is asked:

Q. Ce ta sios?

A. Fear a'tighe

and they all say in a chorus "Buailtear é, buailtear é, buailtear é", and they strike him a few blows.

Other Fugitive Games, following an agrarian mould, show that children in rural places have a natural creative ability for devising their own content for the traditional pattern. Variants can be found in the Gaelic periodical *An Stoc*;[1] here is a translation from the Gaelic:

THE THEFT OF THE GEESE. Yes, one of the oldest girls used to be put to look after the geese, that is, the group of children; another was appointed Woman of the House, and another the Fox. The Woman of the House would then leave home and when the Fox found that she was gone, he would steal a goose. The Woman would then return and begin counting her geese, 1, 2, 3, etc. "I had (17) geese here this morning. Now I have only (16). Where's the other?" The Goosegirl: "The Fox took it with him!" The Woman would then give her a tap with her stick, saying "Take good care to mind the rest, now, and guard them from the Fox." But when she went away again the Fox would come and sweep off with another goose. She would repeat her actions: "Another of my fine geese gone . . ." and so on, until the Fox had stolen all the geese. Next she would go together with the Goosegirl in search of the flock till they

[1] February–March 1924.

found them wherever the Fox had hidden them. Then they would ALL go and chase the Fox, who would run off as fast as he could and they after him, and they shouting "Soliu, soliu!" "Fox! catch the Fox!" When they caught him they would each slap him, saying "Take care you don't steal the geese again!"

LITTLE SHEEP: A BOY'S GAME. Two of the strongest of the boys were appointed shepherds. One had to mind the flock, the other to attend to his farm. The first would range the children at his back, the first one clasping his waist, and each successive one in Indian file. Then No. 2 would come and say "Shepherd, count your lambs". No. 1 says: "Why am I to, master?" No. 2: "Because one of my fine wethers has disappeared." No. 1 then counts his lambs and pretends that there is one more than there actually was. Then the first 'lamb' would stretch out his foot, asking "Is *that* your wether?" "It is not", from No. 2. The second lamb does the same, and so on till they come to the last lamb. Then Shepherd No. 2 would say "*That's* my wether". Next there follows a struggle, No. 1 trying to keep the lamb and saying "You won't get it", while No. 2 tries to get it.

From such as these it can be seen how the pursuit action and the act of battle or contest are frequently combined in one and the same game. Remarkable in this class is the game of *Pick-a-back*, very popular throughout Ireland and a survival of the ancient tourneys, a delight to small boys.

Carleton[1] mentions these in his famous description of "An Irish Hedge School", an account in which the historical atmosphere is portrayed with all the vivid detail of a modern documentary-film scenario.

> . . . the floor, which is only swept every Saturday, is strewed over with tops of quills, pens, pieces of broken slate, and tattered leaves of *Reading Made Easy*, or fragments of old copies. In one corner is a knot engaged in "Fox and Geese", or "The Walls of Troy" on their slates; in another, a pair of them (i.e. scholars) are "*fighting bottles*", which consists of striking the bottoms together, and he whose bottle breaks first, of course, loses. Behind the master is a third set, playing "Heads and Points", a game with pins. Some are more industrially employed in writing their copies. . . .

[1] *Traits and Stories of the Irish Peasantry.*

Warlike games have always appealed to boys above a certain age, and nowhere more than in the places of Ireland near where actual battles or sieges took place. The persistence of the Martial Games has been most extraordinary. It is a subject which has received little attention from historians or folklorists, although it offers fascinating scope for those who would ordinarily try to probe the aggressive instincts of the human race. Foreign elements are more quick to respond to this behaviour than in

emulating other customs of the ancient country in which they would take root. For example, it is of considerable historical interest to note that the Huguenot community in the south of Ireland formed a branch of the Irish Volunteer Corps in 1780 for their children who delighted in playing at fighting games[1] among themselves.

ROMAN SOLDIERS

The Game of Conquest most widespread among English children is that known as *The Roman Soldiers*, in which the players divide up into two equal sides. Standing in two lines, *A* (the Romans) and *B* (the English), they face each other a few yards apart, and begin to exchange parley in sung verses alternately. Both sides then stand still, point their left arms at each other and

[1] *Ulster Journal of Archæology*, vols. VI and VII.

shout "Shoot! Bang! Fire!", and then engage in a fight. After a general scuffle, both sides form a ring and walk round, singing and going through the various actions described in the verses. The antiquity of this game is fairly evident from the text. Fragments of the "words-of-command" appear to have crept into some of the street rhymes referred to in other chapters.

Just as the Roman Invasion of Britain is remembered in this game, so the British brought it with them to several cities. In garrison towns like Tipperary, a version has been noted in which the opening challenge runs:

Are you ready for a fight?
For we are Irish soldiers,

a nice adaptation made by the children themselves.

Of course, the same game is reflected in the pattern of *Cowboys and Indians*, *Gangsters and G-Men* and other modernisations. That it came to Ireland by way of the English soldiery is the case contended here, and its persistence in Dublin, notably in the slums, is due to the influence of English rule. O'Casey, in fact, in his quotation of the game,[1] reveals a local Irishism in the

[1] *I Knock at the Door*, p. 115.

very opening line, i.e. "We are ready for to fight . . ." The extract reads:

> . . . a green sash to go across his breast; blue belt round his waist; and many coloured strips waving gaily from his cap. Then armed with a home-made wooden sword, he turned himself into a warrior, a conqueror of many, bent on battle, free from terror, ready to strike at the first enemy that came near, as he strode along streaming with coloured orders presented to him by Her Majesty Queen Victoria. Whenever a chance came he would share his treasure with a group of Catholic boys, just home from school, decorating them with minor-coloured strips, changing them into soldiers, sergeants, with an ensign carrying a many-hued paper flag, and a drummer bearing on his hip a tin, veiled in strips of yellow and blue, rallying away for dear life, while the boys sang at the top of their voices,
>
> *We are ready for to fight,*
> *We are the Rovers;*
> *We are all brave Parnell's men,*
> *We are his gallant soldiers!*
>
> a song Johnny didn't like, for he was afraid that, in some way or another, it had a connection with the Fenians. . . .

Now the vowel conversion of "We are the soldiers", or "We are the Romans" into "We are the Rovers" has a bearing on a song of this class formerly sung in the streets of Belfast by mill-doffers in a truculent mood. "Rovers" means a special type of linen workers. The version, collected by Hugh Quinn, is as follows, the last four lines offering another example of how topicality ousts traditionalism in words to an old tune. They refer to a keenly contested election between Senton, a Nationalist candidate, and Foster, a Unionist, for a seat representing West Belfast in the early nineties. Senton won by a narrow majority:

Do you want to breed a fight
We are the Rovers
For it's if you want to breed a fight
Oh, we're the jolly fine Rovers.

Senton at the head of the poll,
We are the Rovers,
And Foster's looking up his . . .
Oh, we're the jolly fine Rovers.

All these verses preserve the ancient trochaic measure, which was the popular stress of the Roman soldier, and the literary continuity of the original English Singing Game, with its metrical rhythm of *tum-ti tum-ti*, *tum tum tum* enhanced by the beat of the melody, contains all the best qualities of narrative balladry.

(1) *Have you any bread and wine?*
For we are the Romans:
Have you any bread and wine?
For we are Roman soldiers.

(2) *Yes, we have some bread and wine . . .*
For we are the English soldiers.

(3) *Then we will have one cup full*
For we are the Roman soldiers.

(4) *No, you shan't have one cup full*
For we are the English soldiers.

(5) *Then we will have two cups full*
For we are the Roman soldiers.

(6) *No, you shan't have two cups full*
For we are the English soldiers.

(7) *We will tell the Pope of you*
For we are the Roman soldiers.

(8) *We don't care for the Pope or you*
For we are English soldiers.

(9) *We will tell the King of you*
For we are the Romans.

(10) *We don't care for the King or you*
For we are the English.

(11) *We will send our cats to scratch*
For we are the Romans.

(12) *We don't care for your cats or you*
For we are the English.
We will send our dogs to bite . . .
For we are the English.

(13) *We don't care for your dogs or you*
For we, etc.

(14) *Are you ready* for a fight?
For we are the Romans.

(15) *Yes, we're ready* for a fight
For we, etc.

FIGHT TAKES PLACE

(16) *Now we've only got one arm . . .*
For we are the Roman/English.

(17) *Now we've only got one leg . . .*
For we are, etc.

(18) *Now we've only got one eye, etc.*

(19) *Now we've only got one ear, etc.*

In some versions, at the sixteenth verse, the two sides, instead of fighting, join hands and dance round in a ring, singing as follows:

Then we'll join in a merry ring
For we are the Roman/English
Then we'll join in a merry ring,
For we are Roman/English soldiers.

Gomme devotes some pages to a series of variants of an English game called *We are the Rovers*, but the above version is taken from Cecil J. Sharpe's collection in No. 1109 of *Novello's School Songs* (London).

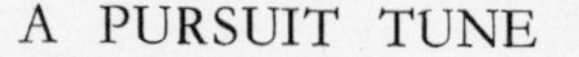

A PURSUIT TUNE

THE SIGNAL FOR STARTING A RACE

This couplet is used as a signal for starting in a race:

Bell horses, bell horses, what time of day?
One o'clock, two o'clock, three and away! (4)

HOGMANAY

Rise up, guidwife, and shak yer feathers,
An dinna think that we are beggars;
We are but bairnies come tae play,
Rise up and gie's oor Hogmanay.
Oo'r ffet's caul, oor shin's thin;
Gie us a piece, an lat us rin!

A SCOTTISH RHYME

When Yule comes, dule comes,
Cauld feet and legs;
When Pasch comes, grace comes,
Butter, mulk and eggs.

Yule's come and Yule's gane,
And we hae feasted weel;
Sae Jock maun tae his flail again,
An Jenny tae her wheel.

February

THE FOCUS ON STONE AND BONE AND BALL

Brings the gradually lengthening daylight which is put to good use in the seasonal urge to hop, leap and move the arms and legs to rhythmic games. Ball Games are the favourite and apart from such popular types as *Donkey* and *Queenie*, you can invent words and tunes for *Hopping*, *Ball-against-the-Wall* and *Ball Beds*. Throwing *Jackstones* (or *Fivestones*) and *Knucklebones* is also the custom now.

Many games have arisen out of rituals connected with the tree. In pre-Christian ritual the tree held a sacred position. Next to the tree in importance was the stone, *petros*, *la pierre*. Before the Greek and Roman sophisticated Ball Games (7) developed, it was the magic of stones from which throwing and tossing originated. In pagan temples, Druidic dolmans, in the erection of altar or dwelling-place, for the weapon or the utensil, concerning the ceremonies of Death and Burial, in cults of pacification, divination, in the practice of exorcision and black magic, in customs relating to Marriage and Birth, the employment of stones has occasioned a vast body of scholastic research. For every application, size, shape and function, reference can be made at museums and libraries. In a chapter on "Foundations and Sacrifices"[1] Bett alludes to the more interesting standard works by authorities on primitive culture.

Saintyves,[2] dealing with the appropriation by the Christian Church of stone-worshipping rituals, writes that ". . . ces réunions païennes se prolongent beaucoup plus tard qu'on l'imagine, soit auprès des pierres, soit auprès des sources. L'Église les traita d'assemblées diaboliques. Les cérémonies qu'on y accomplissait pour les biens de la terre devrinent, à ses yeux, des œuvres des magiciens et des sorciers!" He goes on to narrate, as evidence of the stone-worshipping cults in Normandie, that

[1] *Origin of Games*, Chap. IV, p. 99. [2] *Les Liturgies Populaires*, pp. 16, 17.

"... dans le Bocage normand, non loin de la Chapelle au Cornud, on rencontre, au hameau du Hamel-Auvray, une grande quantité des pierres druidiques allignées en allées...."

It was Lawrence G. Gomme who, in the sphere of ethnology proper, first claimed that these ceremonials formed an integral part of the social habits of the Brythonic Celts (as he termed them) after, as well as before, they settled in the mountainous regions of the British Islands. These social patterns left an indelible impression on the subsequent forms of amusement and communal recreations. In Great Britain, it can be shown that certain ancient magico-ritualistic ceremonies survive in children's games *only*. Yet to this day, in Ireland, survivals, as folk beliefs and superstitions, have held fast among adults, and still persevere. The considerable collection of recent material concentrated in the archives of the Irish Folklore Commission bears out this fact. And as early as 1866, Kennedy[1] was remarking that "... Pagan magicians handed down their sorcery to their quasi-Christian successors". In the same work he quotes a local legend about the placing of stones on a cairn, during the funeral of a child, as evidence of the supernatural attributes of tree and stone (a duality which in Joyce's word-play on the Irish mythos, in *Anna Livia Plurabelle*, recedes into *stem and stone*, Shem and Shawn, the male and female principle, static and fluid).

And so, with their deep-rooted significances, these smooth, rounded pebbles also have an æsthetic appeal—for children, especially. Small stones are the playthings of the poor and provide the "props" for make-believe in any game of *House*, or *Shops*; the currency for juvenile gambling, on any brick-strewn building-site or blitzed lots. In country places where they play at *Ball in the Cap*, it is stones that are employed. They provide the items of amusement in *Duck at the Table*, which Patterson tells us[2] was "a boy's game played with round stones and a table-shaped block of stone".

In Ireland they used to play a game actually called *Stones*. A full account of it appears in the *Dublin Folklore Journal* as follows:

> A circle of stones is formed according to the number of players, generally 5 or 7, on each side. One of the out party stands in the

[1] *Legendary Fictions of the Irish Celts* (1866), p. 163.   [2] *County Down Glossary*.

centre of the circle, and lobs at the different stones in rotation; at each hit a player gives, all his side must change stations, in some places going round to the left, in others to the right. The stones are defended by a hand or a stick, according as the ball or stick is lobbed. All the players are 'out' if the stone is hit, or the ball or stick caught or one of the players hit while running. In different counties or places these games are more or less modified.

This excerpt has more than just academic interest, because it gives ample evidence that the ancient Irish game of *Stones* was a direct ancestor of cricket. Anglo-Saxon pride might not welcome such an ancestry (12), for cricket has come to be regarded as a product peculiar to the English tradition, and even encyclopædiae underline the exclusively English character of the game. But the view that *Stones* was a direct ancestor of Cricket is supported by Kinahan, a close friend of Alice B. Gomme and an observer whose reports she treated with respect.

Chronicling what would appear to have been the period 1830 to 1840, he remarks:

I have seen these games played over half a century ago with a lob-stick, but of later years with a ball, long before a cricket club existed in Trinity College, Dublin, when that game was quite unknown in a great part of Ireland. *At the same time, they may have been introduced by some of the earlier settlers*, and afterwards degenerated into the games (Stones) mentioned above; but I would be inclined to suspect that the Irish are the primitive games, *they having since been incorporated into cricket*. At the present day these games are nearly everywhere succeeded by cricket but often in a very primitive form, the wickets being stones set on end, etc. (Italics are inserted.)

There can be no doubt that most of the modern English team games derive from Celtic origins. Football in particular has a long history among the Celtic peoples. If Kinahan's reports are acceptable the team idea and pattern of test-match cricket are simply a refinement upon the ancient Gaelic lobbing-game of *Stones*.

Another similar Irish game mentioned by Gomme is *Lobber*, in one respect reminiscent of *Rounders*. This is her description of it:

There are three or more players on each side, two stones or holes as stations, and one Lobber. The Lobber lobs either a stick about three inches long or a ball (the ball seems to be a new institution, as a stick was always formerly used), while the batsman defends the stone or hole with either a short stick or his hand. Every time the

stick or ball is hit, the boys defending the holes or stones must change places. Each one is out if the stick or ball lodges in the hole or hits the stone; or if the ball or stone is caught; or if it can be put in the hole, or hits the stone while the boys are changing places. The game is also played with two Lobbers that lob alternately from each end. The game is won by a certain number of runs. . . .

Another cricket game played until quite recently was *Tip and Run*. This game introduces *Stones* into the pattern of a Pursuit Game, as is the case with *Fox and Geese* referred to by Kennedy. Regarding the latter, Micklewaith[1] remarks on a piece of illuminating historical data: ". . . of having found figures of this game cut in the cloister benches of Gloucester Cathedral, and elsewhere, and there are several in the twelfth-century tomb at Salisbury, and in Norwich Castle." Micklewaith points out that for the past four hundred years, cloisters all over England have been open passages—where there generally have been schoolboys about. "These play-boards were likely to have been left behind them, for if they were of a later date they would not be found distributed in monastic cloisters with respect to the monastic arrangement—and we do find them thus."

The *Tip and Run* version is still played, and here is a modern version of it (June 1941):

> A large flat stone is placed standing on its edge supported behind by a stick, or other stones. The ball is bowled towards the wicket from a smaller stone placed flat on the ground several yards away. The batsman hits it and runs to tip the flat stone which he must touch with his bat. Fielding is as in cricket. The player who puts the batsman out, wins. This is a game of individualistic prowess. The player who makes most runs, wins. There is none of the team spirit.

Another variety of *Stone* game, from the same village, is pronounced "Quates" although spelt "Quoits":

> A large flat stone is placed in position. Each player in turn throws three or four smaller flat stones toward it, from a line drawn on the ground with a boot-heel. The large stone is known as the 'Jock'. If a stone remains on the 'Jock' after being thrown, it counts as two points. If there are, say, five players, the owners of the five stones nearest the 'Jock' get one point each. One player may get all the points. The distance is measured with a straw from the nearest point of quoit or 'Jock'. Many arguments arise over the measurements! The play continues till the total, formerly agreed on, is reached.[2]

This game has something in common with the *Cockshy*, or *Cockshot*, Game. Played by children on the sea-shore, an oblong

[1] *Indoor Games of Schoolboys in the Middle Ages.* [2] Michael O'Cullinane, Skibbereen.

stone is used as a pivot for a series of smaller ones, forming a pyramid. Aiming skilfully seems to be the chief object of this amusement.

Skittles is another country game which has outlived its vogue among city children.

From playing with stones, it is not a far development to games played with a ball (9). The Gaelic word "Caid" refers to the type

of ball used in the Kerry peninsulas over a hundred years ago. It was made of certain cured skins from farm animals, with a natural bladder inflated within. It was not round. Rather was it oval in shape. In the field game, boughs of trees, bent into the shape of an arch, were used as goals. In the cross-country variety, the object was to take the ball from one parish to another, i.e. to take *An Caid* home. An exhaustive essay on the traditional game of *Caid* has been written by the Reverend W. Ferris, of Glenfesk, Killarney.

Yet football has an older tradition in north-east Ireland. It was played on the banks of the Boyne as early as 1660. A description of a match played in the town land of Fennor, on the southern bank of the Boyne river, occurs in a very excellent poem by Seumas Dall Mac Cuarta, born in 1647. Perhaps the earliest account of a football match ever to appear in print was the epic poem written by Matt Concanen (the Elder) in the year 1720. "If not a gem of literature," remarks a pseudonymous writer in the journal *Gaelic Football*, "it is a kaleidoscopic picture of football as played in Finglas, North Dublin, 220 odd years ago." The same author states:

> On the frozen Liffey in 1741 a football match was played on the ice. Drumcondra, in 1774 as in 1884, was a football centre. In the meadows of the Midlands and South, a crude football was popular right up to the middle of the nineteenth century. But competition was sporadic—just annual inter-parish holiday affairs.

Relating to the Celtic origin of football, Gomme quotes a memoir by an octogenarian from Lampeter, which bears a fascinating sidelight on its possible migration to Britain from Ireland:

> In North Wales we called the ball *Bel Troed*, and it was made with a bladder covered with *Cwd Tarw*. In South Wales it was called *Bel Ddu*, and was usually made by the shoemaker of the parish, who appeared on the ground on Christmas Day with the ball under his arm. The *Bros*, it should be mentioned, occupied the high ground of the parish. They were nicknamed "Paddy Bros" from a tradition that they were descendants of Irish people who settled on the hills in days long gone by. The *Blaenaus* occupied the lowlands, and, it may be presumed, were pure-bred Brythons . . . the match began about midday, after the church service . . . then rich and poor, *Blaenau* and *Bro*, assembled on the turnpike road, which divided the highlands and the lowlands. . . .

The choice of Christmas Day for the match is noteworthy for the reason that this was the day on which the communal *Caid* was played in Ireland, when, as we are assured, "it is played very fair and with good humour".

* * * * *

Striking a ball with the hand against a wall was a common form of amusement in England in the fourteenth and fifteenth centuries. And the game of *Fives*, involving the use of a Fives Court, is one of the forms in which it has come down to us, relatively unchanged, today. *Fives* took its name from its French originator, *jeu de paume* (now used of tennis), referring to the five fingers of the hand. A statute in the reign of Edward III forbids

2 Skating

3 Whip-top on Frozen Pond

4 Sliding Upon the Ice
From a print after Francis Hayman, 1862

5 Bat and Ball
Fourteenth century

6 Girls Juggling

BALL GAMES

7 Girl with Ball
After a painting by Yankel Adler (*Gimpel Gallery*)

8 "One, two, three, a-leary . . ."
(*Photo Z. Glass*)

the game on the score that its popularity was interfering unduly with the (more necessary) practice of archery.

Tennis, on the other hand, is the most ancient of our surviving Ball Games. Supposedly invented in Italy during the Middle Ages, it came to England, as did so many fashionable sports, via France (10). In Chaucer's day, it had become quite a popular pastime.

OTHER BALL GAMES

Gomme records a report from a Mrs. Lincoln of a game called *Ball in the Decker*. "A row of boys' caps are set up against a wall.

A ball was thrown always into the last cap." This is a combination of Ball and Pursuit Game. O'Casey[1] likewise writes of its being a much favoured game among street-players in Victorian Dublin:

> ... "Let's have Ball in the Decker, first," said Johnny, "an' afterwards Duck in the Grawnshee; an' I'll be last in both, for the sake of the game."
>
> Then they all laid their caps in a row at an angle against the wall of a house. They took turns, Touhy first and Johnny last, trying to roll a ball into one of the caps, the player doing his best to avoid it

[1] *I Knock at the Door*, p. 117.

rolling into his own. When the ball rolled into a cap, the owner ran over to his cap, the rest scattering in flight, caught the ball up, and flung it at a boy nearest and easiest to hit. If he missed, a pebble was put in his cap, but if he hit a boy, then a pebble was put in the cap of the boy the ball had struck. The game went on till a boy had six pebbles or more (the number being decided at the beginning of the game). Then the boy with the six pebbles in his cap had to stand by the wall, and stretch out his arm, and press the back of his hand firm against the bricks. Then each boy, with a hard half-solid ball, had six shots at the outstretched hand; each aiming at hitting it as hard as he could. . . .

Though now obsolete in Ireland, an almost exact equivalent is described in detail by Kennedy[1] as among the sources of "excitement of these playmates of the year 1811 in Rathnure chapel-yard". Kennedy alludes to the game as *Pillar the Hat*, to which he remarks in a footnote: "Never having heard this title applied to the game since the period referred to, we are unable to explain it. Can it be 'Pile (*Pileus*, Cap) or Hat', or 'Ball in the Hat', subject to the usual rubbing or blurring consequent on long use among unlettered people?"

The last phrase has a tremendous interest for us as revealing Kennedy's brilliant investigatory mind grappling here with his sole incursion into the realm of comparative philology as applied to the history of children's games. We shall dwell on the question of "rubbing or blurring" in a later section treating of textual corruptions.

If Irish games have been enthusiastically fostered by other peoples, immigrants are to be thanked for corresponding contributions. For example, the lawn game of *Croquet*, having since become associated with the most genteel of pastimes and people, was introduced by the French Huguenots who settled at Portarlington. It has been known there as *Crookey*. Both at Portarlington and at Kilkee, County Clare, it was played "with wooden crooks and balls fifty years ago (i.e. *circa* 1840), but about 1865 mallets were introduced at Kilkee; subsequently the game was changed to croquet".[2]

[1] *Dublin Univ. Mag.*, November 1862, p. 607.
[2] *Dublin Folklore Journal*, vol. II, pp. 264–5.

BOUNCING-BALL GAMES

Hopping, bouncing and leaping movements are a delight to primitive and savage tribes. The bouncing of a ball has an equally strong rhythmic appeal for children (5). Homer's reference to the white-armed maidens playing ball in the *Odyssey*, VI, suggested that it was a common pastime among Greek children. With them, games of skill, agility and athletic prowess included throwing stones (or balls) at a given target.

These Ball Games appear to be played with more gusto by girls (6) of all ages than by boys, as we shall likewise observe in the case of *Skipping*. Ball Games likewise seem to bear the seasonal feature marking *Skipping*, *Tops*, *Marbles*, *Chestnuts*, *Hopscotch*, and other "crazes" that appear for a definite period, only to give way to others.

A wide range of rhymes has accrued from the incantatory formulæ that accompany several forms of these games. Some are just elaborate games of skill involving (*a*) throwing; (*b*) catching; and (*c*) elimination; for example, the games of *Queenie*, *Donkey*, etc. Here is a description of *Queenie*:[1]

A

A stands with her back to the other players. Any number of players.

A stands holding ball, back turned to other players, who stand at some distance behind. She throws the ball over her head, backwards. If any one of the players succeeds in catching the ball before it falls to the ground, that player replaces *A*. If the ball hops or rolls, and a player catches it and holds it behind her back, saying "Queenie" before *A* sees it, and *A* correctly guesses the holder of the ball, *A* can throw again. If not, the girl who holds the ball replaces *A*.

A *B*
C *D*

Four players stand in each corner of a square. *A* throws the ball to *B*, *B* to *C*, *C* to *D* and *D* to *A*. If one of the players fails to catch the ball she is designated as *D*. If she fails again she is *O*, and so on through the letters of the word *D O N K E Y*. The game continues until one player is "Donkey".

[1] As played in June 1940.

In both town and rural districts, variants occur on this basic pattern.

In the towns, where paved footpaths afford natural playgrounds for the poor and better scope for bouncing, Ball Rhymes are more common than in the country. Games played with bouncing a ball are, roughly classed, as follows: (*a*) Ball against a Wall; (*b*) Other improvised Ball Games; and Ball Beds.

Rhymes are invented to accompany the actions and here are some that I took down from time to time:

(*a*) *Ball against a Wall* (*with Actions and Tricks*) (8)

1. *I heard the King say*
   Quick March!
   Under the Arch!
   Salute to your King!
   Bow to your Queen!
   Sit down, kneel down,
   Touch the ground,
   And a burley-round![1]

2. *Throw up the ball,*
   Let it fall,
   Dickery, one, two,
   Clinkey-bell,
   And burley-round.[2]

3. *Throw up the ball,*
   Let it fall,
   Clappy-clappy,
   Heely-toe,
   Right hand,
   Left hand,
   Swale's mouth
   April, May
   Creadly
   Rooly, fiddle-y,
   And burley-round.[3]

3 (a) Same as (3) with:
   Cheeky, elbow, knee,
   Craddly, Rolly,
   Fiddly and Burley-round.
   O.X.O.[4]

4. *Ala-balla, alla-balla,*
   Who has got the ball?
   I haven't got it
   In my pocket,
   So you *must have got the ball.*[5]

5. *Saucy Mary won the game*
   And wrapped it up in her
   petticoat tail![3]

(*b*) *Ball-in-the-Beds, or Ball Beds*

Here geometrical figures are drawn on the roadway or pavement or school playground with pieces of crude white chalk or plaster (e.g. in Dublin), or sticks of coloured chalk. They are numbered differently from hopscotch "beds"; varied rules apply. Here are some of the rhymes:

[1] County Antrim, February 1942.
[2] County Derry, February 1942.
[3] North Dublin, December 1941.
[4] County Down, March 1942.
[5] County Down, February 1942.

A Rhyme for Ball-in-the-Beds

LOOBEY LIGHT

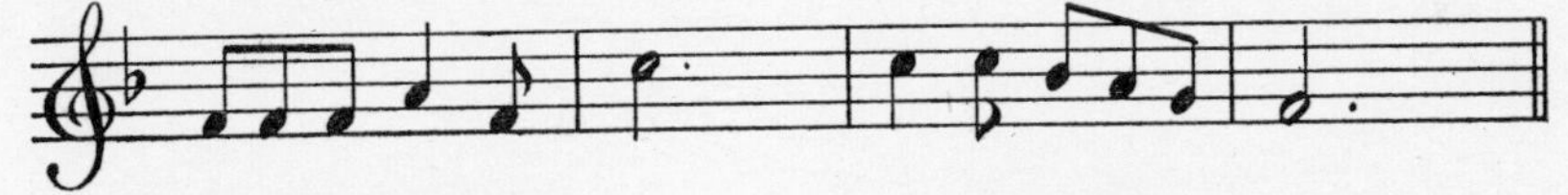

O here we go Loobey Loo
O here we go Loobey Light
Here we go Loobey Loo
All on a Saturday night.

Lift your left leg up,
Put your left leg down,
Shake it a little and shake it a little,
And turn yourself around.

* * * * *

1. *I love coffee, I love tea,*
I love the boys and they love me.
Tell your mother to shut up her tongue
That she had a boy herself when she was young![1]
One, two, three (O'Leary), four, five, six (O'Leary),
On an (O'Leary) morning.

2. *Are you coming (sir)?*
No (sir). Why (sir)?
Because I've got the cold (sir).
Where did you get the cold (sir)?
Up at the North Pole (sir).
What were you doing there (sir)?
Catching polar bear (sir).
How many did you catch (sir)?
One (sir), two (sir), three (sir).[2]

3. *One, two, three O'Leary,*
I spy Miss O'Leary,
Sitting on her bum, O'Leary,
Eating chocolate soldiers.[3]

4. *I've got a bike,*
A Fairy Bike it is,
I can ride it.
Quick march!
Under the arch!
Umply, umply,
Um bum bum.[4]

5. *One, two, three O'Leary,*
I spied my Auntie Seary
Going to the Lucan Dairy
Early in the morning.[5]

6. *Bum, bum, bailey-O,*
Two to one the barbel-O,
Barbel-O, barbel-O,
Bum, bum, Bailey-O.[6]

7. *Billy Boland*
Biscuit baker
Ballybough bridge![7]

[1] Belfast, February 1942.
[2] Kilkeel, County Down, February 1942.
[3] Patrick Street, North Dublin, 1939.
[4] County Down, 1942.
[5] Dublin, 1930–5.
[6] Dublin, 1939.
[7] Ringsend, Dublin and Kilkeel, County Down, 1941–2.

8. *Here we go hoobee hoobee*
Here we go hoobee hight
Here we go hoobee hobee
Ev'ry Saturday night.
Put your left hand in!
Put your right hand out!
Shake it a little, and
Shake it a little, and
Turn yourself about![1]

9. *Charlie Chaplin went to France*
To teach the ladies how to dance:
This is the way he taught them:
Heel, toe, under you go!
Charlie Chaplin ran a mile,
He took a penny from a child,
When the child began to cry,
Charlie Chaplin said good-bye!

10. *Aonder, do-der, tri-der,*
God bless me (sir)
Protect me (sir)
I ask you,
A-bask you,
A back-to-front
And a rolly stunt
My father works in the G.P.O.
General Post Office![2]

11. *Parnell*
Went to the well,
He never forgot his soap and towel,
Washed his face and combed his hair,
Said his prayers
And went to bed.[3]

12. *Clipsy, clapsy,*
Sidesy, backsy,
Right hand, left hand, both hands,
Wee burley, big burley, dash.[4]

What strikes the ear of the uninitiated as merely bits of sonorous jingle, or baby-language formed from invented onomatopœic words denoting, say, the clapping of hands or the thudding of a ball against wood or plaster with its insistent tempo, are, in reality, technical terms. Technical in the sense that they interpret specific actions or physical achievements and are accepted as the structural conventions in following out the pattern of a game. A remarkable feature about all this is that the same sets of rules, words and rhythms in ball-beds recur in places where there is no evident traffic in juvenile ideas of any kind. The language spreads mysteriously: the terms become part of the child's vocabulary, as does (the more fleeting) film-slang that finds its way through comics or adult catch-phrases into the innermost places of communal life. But I was intrigued to discover in villages as remote from each other, as Randalstown in the County Antrim is to Crosshaven in the County Cork such words as hoobie, claimy, clappy, burley, bumble, arch, ask, bask,

[1] Dublin, 1940 (general).
[2] Dublin, 1941.
[3] County Armagh, February 1942.
[4] County Down, 1942.

back, rolly, etc. Each of their variants in the different dialects belongs to this esoteric vocabulary.

Take the recurrence of the mnemonic o-x-o. It has given rise to curiosity among those who have bothered to decipher the jargon. I should say that it occurs where it does owing to the necessity for ending a hopping "lap" on the vowel "o". Thus we get another equivalent in the form of G.P.O. (see p. 34, No. 10).

In parts of Ireland they still play a game involving the chalking on the ground of another curious shape. It resembles a snail-shell, and is marked off in numerical values. They dice at random for a number. Say "four" comes up. This awards four "rings" along the spiral track to the child who throws four, and the value chalked on the fourth section is credited to the thrower. Each child takes a turn and at the end of an agreed period the largest total wins.

To the throwing of the dice and the adding-up of the totals (usually chalked likewise on the pavement or roadway) they intone a special rhyming ditty that goes like this:

Chip chop cherry
All the men from
Londonderry
Cannot climb the
Highest wall,
Chip, chop, cherry.

JACKSTONES

Jackstones, played with three or four small stones that are thrown up in the air and caught again, seems to have been a very ancient game, as the stones have been found in the *crannogs* (lake-dwellings), in some hole near the fireplaces, similar to where they are found in a cabin at the present day [*circa* 1880]. An old woman, or another player, at the present time, puts them in a place near the hob when they stop their game and go to do something else. . . .[1]

G. H. KINAHAN

What hucklebones[2] were to the children of English towns and cities, jackstones have been, and still are, to the children of rural Ireland. *Hucklebones*, or *Knucklebones*, as a game, still features among the customs of island savage tribes, and forms the subject

[1] *The Folklore Journal*, vol. II, p. 226. [2] Played with sheep's trotters.

of much archæological investigation by authorities on primitive customs. Thus Falkener, in his *Games Ancient and Oriental*,[1] reproduces a hieroglyphic sent to him in a letter from S. Buch, as follows: "This ancient Egyptian word", he writes, "means CHESS:

the dead, or their spirits, were supposed to play it in their future state. In the Greek or Roman Elysium, the dead play at TALI or knuckle-bones. . . ."

* * *

F for Fig, I for Jig,
and N for knuckle bones,
I for John the waterman
and S for sack of stones.

* * *

Knucklebones is a very ancient game indeed. It originated, in all probability, in what is now Japan and was introduced from Asia into Europe by the Romans. Roman soldiers and colonists spread it throughout the Empire as they popularised so many other similar games.

Yet, surprisingly enough, it does not appear to have been played in Ireland. Or, if it was, it has become long since obsolete. The reason advanced here as a possible theory regarding its failure to enjoy popularity in Ireland is that this was a game of a sedentary nature, one in which there was little exertion, or action, involved. It has always been popular among London children, though less frequently found in Dublin (usually derived from English sources), and Norman Douglas includes rhymes connected with this game in his anthology. It is quite probable that the following Singing Rhyme has its origin in this ancient game:

Nick nack Paddy Whack
Give a dog a bone
This old man came rolling home

[1] p. 18, 1892.

This old man
He played one,
He played nick nack on my drum
Nick nack Paddy Whack
Give a dog a bone
This old man came rolling home.[1]

It may, on the other hand, be an entirely separate game. According to Professor Atwell,[2] *Hucklebones* was introduced into Europe from Asia by the Romans and was spread throughout the countries which formed the Empire by means of Roman soldiers and colonists. But it was a very different game, also proceeding from Asia, which took root in this country where it still obtains, namely the game of *Jackstones*.

Under the name of *Fivestones*, another form of this game has been played in rural England, for Gomme gives a full account of it. She also quotes a report from Kinahan as follows: "The Japanese version of the game TEDAMA (Handballs) came to America, where its evidence in Boston is recorded by Newell as 'OTADAMA', or 'Japanese Jacks'. . . ."[3]

Kinahan contends that both *Fivestones* and *Otadama* are branches from the same root. Hence, as Gomme concludes, we have here an example of a game which, having preserved its essential characteristics for thousands of years, has fairly

[1] Dublin, November 1939. Successive verses have two. . . shoe, three. . . tree, four. . . door, etc. [2] *Notes and Queries*, 8th series, vol. IV, p. 201. [3] *Games*, pp. 190–3.

circumscribed the globe, so that the two currents of tradition, westward from Europe and eastward from Asia, have met in America!

That it is one of the oldest games played with stones there can be little doubt, and that it has a separate Gaelic tradition, with a distinctive Gaelic name, is a matter of no little significance. A writer in *Irisleabhar na Gaedhilige*[1] makes a brief query: "In Aran I have seen children play *Sgreaga*: but I do not know the words. I have also seen a game called *Asal*, played with two hands. . . ." He must have aroused interest, for in a later number of the journal another contributor wrote an article citing three games as played in Aran Island: (1) *Prisoner's Base*; (2) *Gor*; and (3) *Sgreaga*. He includes the rules for (3) in Gaelic, as follows:

> The game of *sgreaga* has to be played with one hand, and if you fail in any trick of the game, another person begins. *Sgreaga* and *creaga* are the same thing, i.e. little stones, and you need five of them.
>
> A. 1. Put down the five stones on the palm of your hand (while doing the trick, say "Five!"): throw them up in the air, turn your hand so that the stones, in coming down, fall on the back of your hand. 2–8. Do the same trick seven times running, saying "Fifteen!", "twenty!" or ("no lie"), "Twenty-five", "thirty", "thirty-five", "forty", "forty-five".
>
> B. 1. Throw the five stones on the ground, pick up one and throw it into the air, then take two others, and, as the first one falls, catch it. Do the same with the first stone and the other two. (Say "one for churn.") 2. Throw down the five stones, throw one of them up, take three others and catch the other as it comes down ("two for churn"). 3. Throw up one of them, take the other four and catch the first as it falls ("three for churn").
>
> C. 1. Throw down four stones, throw the fifth up in the air, pick up two of the four, strike them on your knee without letting them fall, then catch the other as it comes down ("One for striking knee"). 2, 3. The same trick twice ("Two for striking knee", "Three for striking knee").
>
> D. The same, but strike your chest ("One for striking chest", etc.).

[1] Seumas Mac Cuarta: Imirt-na-Boinne.

E. The same, but strike your other palm ("One for striking palm", etc.).

F. Strike the stones on the ground before you catch the one in the air ("One for striking the ground", etc.).

G. Put two stones in your mouth, throw another in the air, pick up two from the ground, put your hand into your mouth, and take out the two that were there, then catch the one in the air. The same trick three times ("One for striking the mouth", etc.).

H. Your two hands in this trick. Rest the tips of the fingers of your left hand on the ground, held apart so that there is a gap, or door, between each two fingers, i.e. four doors. Now put a stone in front of each door. (The stones are likened to donkeys passing through doors.) Now begin with the furthest stone, and shove the stones in under your hand. Take the fifth stone in your right hand, throw it up in the air; take the other four stones in your left hand and catch the falling stone in your left hand ("One for Donkey", etc.). The same trick three more times. That is the game of *sgreaga* or jackstones.

Ridicule probably accompanies this last movement, and so offers comparison with the Greek version of *I, Midas*, discussed in another chapter.

Kennedy,[1] that astute observer, does not omit to mention that *Jackstones* occupied pride of place in the catalogue of *divarsions* at the Hedge School in County Wexford:

> Much favoured in their own eyes were the bread-and-milk provided pupils, for *their* play-hour was a full half-hour longer than that of their dinner-seeking comrades. Little time was lost till games were formed. Those of the girls consisted of *Jackstones* (five in number), whose proper handling was certainly a matter of difficulty. The little operator taking the five in hand, tossed up one, shed the others on the ground, and caught the liberated one before it fell. If two of the stones were in contact after falling, her hand was out; but if all were separated, she continued to toss the same stone as before in the air, catch up one from the ground, and secure the "skied" stone before it fell. The next stage was to grasp two at a time, and catch the flying stone along with them; and in a later section she caught up the four stones at once, though lying separately. But how

[1] *Dublin Univ. Mag.*, Nov. 1862, p. 609.

she made an arched portal of her middle finger and thumb, tossed one stone in the air, and sent the others one by one through this archway before it (the sky stone) fell, is more than we could describe, as our lady readers understand. . . . The listless little girls of cities seem thoroughly ignorant of this exciting pastime. . . .

9 Forerunner of Handball
Sixteenth century

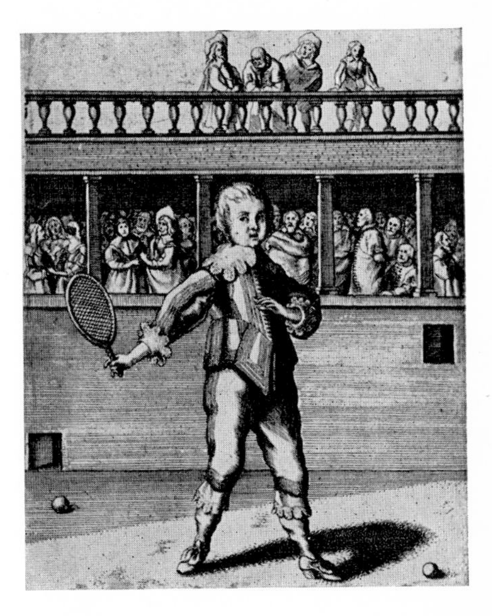

10 "The High Borne Iames,
Duke of York,
playing tennis"

11 Shuttlecock, 1804

12 Village Cricket

13, 14 Hopscotch and Whipping-top
From eighteenth-century engravings

March

Blows in the first fine days of the year. Out come the bits of chalk—for sketching squares and rectangles on the roads and pavements. For, with spring around the corner, focus and

attention are turned to the ground. The games of this month are HOPSCOTCH (13); MIMING GAMES; TOPS (14); and GADGETS.

HECK-A-BEDS

Beds is the conventional equivalent term used by Irish children for the game of *Hopscotch*. Jamieson gives the same term as the Scottish name for this hopping game, also Brockett. In parts of rural Ireland it used to be known as *Scotch Hop*. Twice in *Poor Robin's Almanack* we find reference to playing at "Scotch-hoppers". In the 1667 edition, Verses to the Reader announce "The time when school-boys should play at Scotchhoppers". And the popularity of the game among adults occurs in the same periodical for 1707: "Lawyers and Physicians have little to do this month, and therefore, they may (if they will), play at Scotch hoppers. Some men put their hands into people's pockets open, and extract it clutched, of that beware. But counsel without a cure is a body without a soul."

Again, in 1740, the horoscope is cast in realistic terms:

> The fifth house tells ye whether whores be sound or not; when it is good to eat tripes, bloat herrings, fry'd frogs, rotten eggs, monkeys' tails buttered, or an ox liver well stuck with fish-hooks; when it is the most convenient time for an old man to play at Scotch-hoppers among the boys. In it also is found plainly, that the best armour of proof against the fleas is to go drunk to bed. . . .

In Gomme's detailed analysis of the history of this game the Somersetshire term for it is given as *Hickety-Hackety* 25, and the article kicked from square to square is a piece of tile.

Down the ages, elaborations on the ancient rules have accrued. In Dublin, there are four distinct varieties played. In Bandon, West Cork, it is played under the name of *Pignet* with the foot, the hand, *and* the head. Piccy, or Piggy, is also the name used in Dublin for the article kicked along the ground. It may be a stone, or a fragment of a slate or earthenware vessel, or an empty boot-polish tin.

A book on Old London gives an ingenious explanation of the origin of the term "Hopscotch" as played among London children:

> All the street child's usual stock-in-trade, in the way of toys, is chalk (for drawing those incessant white squares on the pavement), perhaps a few worn marbles and a selection of old buttons. The chalked squares, of course, refer to the ancient game of hop-scotch, so called because the player trying to get a stone into a square may only hop over the lines which are 'scotched' or 'traced' on the ground. The London children often use, instead of stones, broken bits of

glass or crockery they call 'chaneys', and to own a private 'chaney' is considered, I am told, highly genteel.

Gomme, whose investigation was fairly thorough, accepts the Asiatic origin of the game but omits to make use of orthographic evidence of such a kind as that afforded by the symbol still surviving in the numeration X (instead of 1) which is an ancient Eastern numerical sign. She does, nevertheless, reproduce a graphic diagram of the game and its rules as reported in a variant from Waterville, County Kerry. It may possibly have an independent origin from the forms played in Britain. This variant is known as *Picky*, and is played as follows:

One player commences by winning the toss. The Pick, a small flat stone, is pitched into No. 1 bed. It is then moved out of this place, backwards, across the front line, and not otherwise touching it, or forcing it with one foot, the other foot being kept up: i.e. the player must hop and use the foot on the ground to strike the Pick. No line must be touched. If this happens, or if the Pick, when being driven towards the pitching line, gets away otherwise than across the front line, the player is 'Out' and the next boy goes in. All the beds are done likewise and all must then be done in a reverse way, beginning with No. 10. The first player to complete the game wins.

It was an unusual oversight for Gomme to have missed Kennedy's reference[1] of 1862 to the Wexford variant of *Heck-a-Beds*. This is as follows:

City flaneurs may occasionally observe eccentric figures chalked on the flags, and little 'jackeens' performing unintelligible antics with their feet and an oyster shell in and out through the labyrinth. He will also hear the word *porridge* occasionally used; but as to what constitutes one party a winner, and another a loser, he will probably be as much in the dark as we are at this moment, after more than a quarter of a century's study of the operation. Rustic boys had a like game, which they called Heck-a-Beds, but which was easily understood and highly interesting. Two long parallel lines were joined at one end by a curve, and at the other by a right line; two diagonals, so to say, crossed the figure near the curve, and lines about a foot and a half asunder, and at right angles to the long walls, connected these walls through their length. One party having won first turn,

[1] *Dublin Univ. Mag.*, Nov. 1862, p. 609.

standing at the square end, pitched a circular slate (three inches in diameter) to a bed formed by the curve and the furthest connecting line. If it rested in the clear space without touching a boundary line, he hopped on one leg into every bed, rested his two soles in the triangular beds when he attained them. And getting into the next triangular bed, and then the end one, still hopping, he kicked the slate before him down to the end. If he succeeded in driving it over the furthest line without it, or his right foot, having rested for a moment on any one of the lines, that bout was successful; and then he won the other beds, in succession, proceeding in the same way. But if he shoved the disc over either of the long parallel boundaries, or if it rested for a moment on a line, or if his foot touched one of the lines, he forfeited that trial and his rival took his turn. When the slate had been pitched into every bed, and successfully kicked back, and out over the end boundary, the game was won. . . .

Obviously there is a wealth of ritualism in the pattern of the game, especially in the representation of the compartments, i.e. geometrical rectangles or portions thereof. It is easy to imagine the avenues for speculation that have fascinated scholars and folklorists, who, between them, have theorised about and explored almost every conception of the After-life and its varying mythologies. From Hades and the ancient Egyptian tomb-world, human analogy has ranged through the Christian postulates which claim these "boxes" represent Purgatory, Limbo, Heaven and Hell. Whatever their last implication, now lost in a stratification of several systems, it would certainly appear that originally the design sprang from ancient Asiatic beliefs and the doctrine that the soul and body undertake different journeys, whether in this, or in other worlds-to-be.

Anthropologists and zoologists who have made a special study of primitive peoples have shown that one of their favourite natural sports are hopping and leaping and jumping movements. Culin notably in his *Korean Games* and *Games of the North American Indians* has thoroughly dealt with their totemistic associations; whereas Mabel J. Reany in a university thesis[1] has examined the history of games among savages. They have both shown that one of the most generally-found hopping games is a form of *Leap-Frog*.

[1] *The Psychology of the Organised Group Game.*

15 Spinning Tops
From an eighteenth-century drawing

16 Le Toupis
From a French engraving of the nineteenth century

17 Winter Scene, with whip-tops
After Brueghel

18 Illuminated Detail
from *Roman d'Alexandre*, 1344, by Jehan de Grise

19 Coiling the String

A traditional schoolboy game, Leap-frog, still enjoys a never-failing popularity in town and country alike. In some places it is called *Frog-jump*.

Another game of this class is *Hop-Skip-and-Run* (37), or *A-Hop-a-Skip-and-a-Jump*, a formal athletic pattern.

Gomme gives a report[1] from Mrs. Lincoln of Dublin referring to the existence there of a game called *Cutch-a-Cutchoo*, with the following description: "Children clasp their hands under their knees in a sitting posture, and jump thus about the room. The one who keeps up longest wins the game."

That this peculiar pastime must have been also the delight of indecorous grown-ups is apparent from a paragraph in the periodical *Notes and Queries*,[2] in which a contributor, "E. D.", comments: "This amusement was fashionable sixty years ago, and from the low dresses worn then by the ladies it was considered indecent. . . ." He gives an extract from a satire called *Cutchacutchoo, or The Jostling Innocents* (second edition, Dublin), in which both the game and the posture are mentioned:

Now with lone tremendous cries
Cutchacutchoo
Let each squat down upon her ham,
Jump like a goat, puck like a ram.

Kennedy[3] has an interesting further footnote to his Essay on "The Irish Hedge School":

> A sport akin to leap-frog was conducted thus: A boy, stooping forward, leaned his head against a wall or tree; another, standing behind, rested his chin on the small of his back, and so on with about five players. Then an athlete, taking a run, and resting his hands on the hips of the hindmost, sprung as far forward as he could, and remaining astride, clapped his hands behind and before, and shouted:
>
> *Hubby-hubby-hu*
> *I'm atop o' you,*
> *And very well too!*
>
> Another succeeded, and sat immediately behind him, and so on, till all the cavaliers that could find room were seated. Then the beasts

[1] Vol. I, p. 94. [2] Series 10, p. 17. [3] Ibid., p. 609.

of burden let go holds and unseated the riders, with as much damage and mortification to them as they could contrive.

. . . It remains here to consider these group games as expressions of corporate playing. The essence of games of this kind is the formation of spontaneous groups to carry out a group idea. The characters usually chosen are PIRATES, GANGSTERS, KINGS and QUEENS, and ADVENTURERS, and the material from which these plots are drawn come from boys' and girls' school magazines, fairy tales, nursery rhymes, films, history, and traditional forms. Usually the form of the game is reinforced by the fascination of dressing-up.[1]

MIMING GAMES

Allow yourself to be swept into the spirit of a miming game, and you will agree that such games approximate most nearly to the Greek spirit of drama than do any of the progressive technical experiments of many "little" theatres. They combine (*a*) dramatic narrative; (*b*) miming; and (*c*) a singing of a musical text by members of a chorus, who themselves participate in the playing of the game.

Although the composite game has certainly incorporated portions of other games which dramatise (*a*) Marriage and (*b*) Burial, it is in effect a descendant of a fertility rite, probably of a similar sort to the English game *Oats and Beans and Barley Grow*, of which Bett says: "It may be suggested that there really was a connection between the two motives, by way of the primitive notion of fecundity, but it is more likely that one game in practice has simply blended with another, and borrowed some part of its action and its formula."

This is the way we sow the beans, (*etc.* =)
This is the way we brush our hair, (*ad lib.*)

[1] Lowenfeld, *Play in Childhood*, p. 232 (1935).

That, in its turn, can be shown to have generic ancestors among the children's games both of France and of Italy—for example:

A French version:

Savez-vous planter les choux,
A la mode, à la mode,
Savez-vous planter les choux
A la mode de chez nous?
(In four verses)
(2) *On les plante avec le pied,* (*etc.*)
(3) *On les plante avec les mains* (*etc.*)
(4) *On les plante avec le nez* (*etc.*)

An Italian version:

Pianta la fava la madre Vilana
quando la pianta, la pianta così;
e la pianta a poco, a poco,
l'altro poco rimane così.
E la pianta così;
l'altro poco rimane così.[1]

Films and gangster stories have already crept into the dramatic presentation of such games, but they have coloured scarcely at all the *forms* of the games still played. These are invariably traditional, with, of course, certain instances of adaptation and modification.

A fair example of a Mime Game from England in *The Mulberry Bush* category, which is universally played all over Dublin nowadays is *There was a girl in our School.* The refrain, "and this is the way she went", is illustrated by mime, and is a typical Dublin localism for comme ci and à la mode (French) and così (Italian). Here is the text:

There was a girl in our school, in our school, in our school,
There was a girl in our school,
And this is the way she went.
Then she became a lady, a lady, a lady . . .
Then she became a lady
And this is the way she went.
Then she became a teacher, a teacher, a teacher . . .
Then she got married, married, married . . .
Then she got a baby, a baby, a baby . . .

[1] In six verses.

Then the baby di-ed, di-ed, di-ed . . .
Then she got a donkey, a donkey, a donkey . . .
Then the donkey kicked her, kicked her, kicked her . . .
Then she went to hospital, to hospital, to hospital . . .
Then she was sewing, sewing, sewing . . .
Then the needle pricked her, pricked her, pricked her . . .
Then she died, she died, she died,
And this is the way she went.

It can be seen that the actions attached to this dramatic game cover the whole gamut of human comedy and tragedy and offer great scope for both the imitative genius among children and plentiful food for generating the hormemnemic faculty formulated by Nunn.[1]

Although to the foregoing lines Nunn's theory of hormomnemic values would not strictly apply, the actions of the Old Woman (La Madre Vilana) planting her beans, form an essential part of the play-idea. But there is more to the game than just mimesis alone. There *is* mimesis—in the conscious copying of the adult's behaviour; but there is also illustration, and it is this which the *actions* afford, at times bordering on the comic (as in the donkey theme), or even the caricature (as in the teacher theme). There is, binding together the whole, a sense of unified dramatic narrative; and finally there is choral singing to a prearranged notation of play. Whereas the traditional French and Italian games have a rigid melody, the Dublin variant is either intoned to a singsong chorus, or to a tune like *Nuts in May*.

A Belfast variant comes from Hugh Quinn's collection:

O when I was a lady, a lady, a lady,
When I was a lady, O then, O then, O then!
It was heigh-ho This Way, This Way, This Way,
It was heigh-ho This Way, O then, O then, O then.

[1] See p. 57.

O when we were married, etc. (They kiss in the ring.)
O when I had a baby, etc. (They go through nursing actions.)
O when my baby died, etc. (They commence to weep.)

The kathartitic delight experienced by the children of Belfast for the death of an imaginary infant is further portrayed in a similar tragic theme enacted in a Ring Game, coupled with a remarkably fine melody:

There were two sisters going to school,
All round the Loney, O!
There were two sisters going to school,
Down by the green wood shady, O.
All round the Loney, O!
They met a lady of the land,
'Tis said she had killed her baby, O.

Sister dear, will you take my hand,
All round the Loney, O,
No, we'll not *take your dirty hand,*
Down by the green wood shady, O,
All round the Loney, O,
Though you're a lady of the land:
For you did kill your baby, O.

*   *   *   *   *

A RHYME FOR SHUTTLECOCK AND BATTLEDORE (11)

Shuttlecock, shuttlecock, tell me true,
How many times have I to go through?
One, two, three, four, etc.

A SHUTTLECOCK RIDDLE

Light though my body is and small,
Though I have wings to fly withal,
And though the air may rove,
Yet was I not by others pressed,
In ease and indolence I'd rest,
And never choose to move.
'Tis beating makes me diligent,
When beat and on an errand sent,
I hurry to and fro,
And like an idle boy at school,
Whom nothing but the rod can rule,
Improve at every blow.

The top as a plaything goes back very far in the history of mankind. Greek children certainly played with it. Virgil,[1] describing Amata's fury as she stormed through the city, employs a telling simile:

[1] *Æneid*, vol. VII, pp. 378–9.

Ceu quondam torto volitans sub verbere turbo
Quem pueri magno in gyro vacua atiria circum
Intendi ludo exercent.

Mediæval imagery (18) in poetry and painting, in England and on the continent of Europe, is full of whipping-tops. Pieter Brueghel, the elder, often likes to introduce a realistic note of childish local colour by depicting this form of play (17). Shakespeare invokes, through words given to Falstaff, memories of himself "crawling like snail unwillingly to school" when he says: "Since I plucked geese, played truant, and whipped top, I knew not what 'twas to be beaten, till lately. . . ."

Baring Gould suggested that the top is developed from the spindle employed in weaving; against which Bett prefers to assume that:

> . . . it appears to be more likely connected with the fire-drill. It is not a very far-fetched suggestion that the spindle of the fire-drill, the very purpose of which was to be twirled round rapidly in the hand, or by a thong, was the origin of this particular toy, and that when a boy spins a top he is in a direct line of descent from primitive man twirling his fire-drill to produce flame.

Local names for whipping tops in England, according to Gomme, are "Gully" and "Hoaty". Patterson in the *Antrim and Down Glossary* gives the word "Hoges" as being a boy's game played with "Peeries" (peg-tops), in which the victor is entitled to give a certain number of blows with the spike of his Peerie to the wooden part of his opponent's (19).

In a Gaelic short story appearing in *Irisleabhar na Gaedhilige*[1] the word "Top" is translated as "Tap". There is no clue from

[1] Vol. XI, 1901, p. 113.

the context as to whether the writer is alluding to a definite Gaelic form of the game, however. It is extremely unlikely that the top was popularised in the *Gaeltacht* from any other channels than those by which it came to the rest of Ireland.

Tops are used all over the world. In France the spinning top can be one of two types: first, that which is whipped into motion by winding the string round the grooves; and the second, which is set in motion by an automatic sprocket. Humming tops are termed: "Toupies d'Allemagne: sorte de toupie (16) creuse et percée d'une côté, qui fait du bruit en tournant."[1]

In the Victorian era, tops were to be seen all over England, Scotland and Ireland. Now they appear to have gone out of vogue, although in the back areas of one city a seasonal demand is created by a few faithful shopkeepers who still cater for older customs. There formerly were three types in use: peg-tops, lashing-tops and humming-tops, the last a more degenerate and refined innovation!

Describing a typical scene of this kind, Alison Uttley in her reminiscent chapter "Games and Toys" gives us a delightful cameo of another fast-fading aspect of country things:

> Everywhere there were little boys playing whip-and-top, playing with deep solemnity, with sudden glances at a neighbour's top, and then a clever flick to keep their own in motion, or to make it leap

> and put the other out of action. The whip-lash was quickly wound in the grooves while others watched. There was skill in setting a top. It was steadied upright, and with a sudden jerk the lash was

[1] Larousse.

torn away and off went the gay little teetotum, whirling as happily as a ballet-dancer.

Well has Miss Uttley observed that it is the undertone of muted strings that often makes a ballet scene lodge in the memory, and that it is the music as much as the pirouettes that excite the onlooker. "A well-spun top," she continues, "emitted a hum like a contented bee, lovely to hear. The tops 'went to sleep' spinning so quickly they seemed to be motionless, and they could be lifted by a good spinner, even taken up in a spoon to spin there. When they rolled over and fell on their sides they were said to be dead." And then, with all the sense of a cartoon market-place galvanised suddenly into animated hurley-burley, we get this picture: "To walk down the village road in top time was as difficult as to walk on ice. Tops flew under one's feet, whips curled around the ankles, and little boys looked baleful when somebody touched a large spinning top and made it die. Drivers kept a watchful eye, for the tops dashed out like wild things under the horses' hooves and boys ran after them."

FOUR OLD TOP GAMES

(20–23)

(From an Ancient Toy-book)

1. THE SPANISH PEG-TOP

The Spanish peg-top is made of mahogany, it is shaped somewhat like a pear; instead of a sharp iron peg, it has a small rounded knob at the end. As it spins for a much longer time than the common English peg-top, and does not require to be thrown with any degree of force in order to set it up, it is extremely well adapted for playing on flooring or pavement.

2. THE PEG-TOP

Peg-tops can be purchased at all toy-shops; those which have tolerably long pegs are best for "peg in the ring" as they describe a much larger circle when spinning, and are more likely to swerve out of the ring than those with short pegs, which are generally "sleepers", that is, apt to keep in one spot whilst spinning (15); the latter, however, are exceedingly well adapted for "chip-stone". In winding the cord at the top, it is the best plan to pass

20, 21 Whipping Tops
From eighteenth-century Dutch prints

22 Whipping Tops 23 Peg Tops
From a series of coloured prints, 1804

24 Boys Skipping, *circa* 1800

25 Girls Skipping, 1800

it two or three times round the peg before you commence winding it on the body of the top. Tops made of boxwood are the hardest and best, but they are the most expensive.

3. PEG IN THE RING

A circle of about three feet in diameter should be drawn on the ground, and one player then begins the game by throwing or "pegging" his top into the middle of the ring, and whilst it continues spinning in there, the other players should "peg" their tops at it; if, however, it gets out of the ring, the moment it

ceases spinning and falls, the owner is at liberty to pick it up and peg at any of those still spinning inside the circle. Should any of the tops fall while in the ring, or any of the players be unable to set their tops up, or not "peg" them fully into the ring, they are reckoned "dead", and must be played in the circle for the others to "peg" at; it often happens that five or six "dead" tops are thus in at one time, and that they are all driven out by one cast, without either of them receiving injury; in this case the players begin the game again. If a player can succeed in splitting a top belonging to one of his antagonists he carries off the peg as a token of victory. Sometimes the rules of the game are so modified by previous arrangement that a player is allowed to place a spare top in the ring instead of the one he is playing with. *Peg in the Ring* ought to be played on smooth, firm ground, or gravel; pavement is not at all adapted to it, as the force with which the tops are cast is liable, on so hard a surface, to split them.

4. CHIP-STONE

This game is usually played by two boys only, who each select and use a small roundish pebble, or "chip-stone", as it is termed; it is their aim to procure the bright black stones, which, from having a very even shape, and a beautifully polished surface, are more esteemed than any of the other colours. Two lines should be marked on the ground or pavement, at some distance apart, and the pebbles should be placed on one of them. The peg-tops are next to be set up, and whilst they continue spinning, the players must take them up in wooden spoons (which can be purchased at the toy-shops, and "chip" or cast them at the stones), the design being to drive the latter from one of the bounds to the other. As the tops frequently keep on spinning, even after they have been cast at the stones, the players are allowed to take them up in their spoons, and "chip" again; indeed a skilful player can "chip" three or four times before the tops cease spinning. The player who can send his chip-stone from one boundary-line to the other, in the fewest casts, is the winner.

"TOPS ARE IN."

* * * * *

"What a glorious thing it was when it lay on the table in the firelight! It was made of tid, or perhaps it was silver, a large many-coloured top, shimmering with blue and green, scarlet and purple. All the colours in the world seemed to mingle in its peacock sheen. It was wound up by a piece of string from the string-bag behind the door, wrapped round it just below the wooden knob. It was so easy, anybody could do it. Then it was placed on its point and left to its intricate dance. The hearth-rug was rolled back, the chairs were moved away, when my father wound up the new humming-top. We stood around for every body must have a peep.

It buzzed and hummed as it flew over the stone floor, and to our joy it played a little tune. The music was something ethereal. There were fine reeds in the upper part, which caught the air and made the musical sound. It was one of those magical times of childhood, a moment of pure beauty never to be lost. It comes again when I hear Bizet's ballet music, "The Spinning Top".[1]

WHIPPING TOPS

Whip top! Whip top!
Turn about and never stop!
Monday's top will spin away,
Tuesday's top will sing all day,
Wednesday's top is never slow,
Thursday's top to sleep will go,
Friday's top will dance about,
Saturday's top will tire you out!
Whip top! Whip top!
Spin around and never stop!

[1] *Country Things*, Alison Uttley.

April

Is the time when the Springing-up of the Seed used to be celebrated by the ancients in movements of hopping (35–39), jumping and skipping with a rope made of vine-strands. They have come down to us, with their incantations and bowing of the head, their gesticulations and actions of limbs and body, as SKIPPING GAMES and SWINGING GAMES (28–30).

SWINGING RHYMES (42)

26 French children playing a Team Game at Skipping

27 Italian peasants skipping in the countryside

28 Swinging Indoors. Early seventeenth century

SWINGS IN

AND OUT OF DOORS

29 From a seventeenth-century engraving

30 Swinging contrivances at a Russian Fair, *circa* 1700

See-saw, Margery Daw, (41)
Johnny shall have a new master.
He will have but a penny a day
Because he can't go any faster.

See-saw, sacradown, (40)
Which is the way to London town?
One foot up, the other foot down,
That is the way to London town.

Ride a cock horse
To Banbury Cross
To see a fine lady
On a white horse
Rings on her fingers
And bells on her toes,
She shall have music
Wherever she goes.

SKIPPING

"Imitation bears to mimesis the same relation that conation bears to HORME and memory to MNEME. In all three cases the Greek term describes a general feature of human and animal behaviour, and the corresponding Latin term is limited to those instances in which the activity is conscious," writes Nunn. He advances, as an illustration of the merging of the two by insensible gradations into one, the child who sees her seniors skipping with a rope. "If she too is to become a skipper, as undoubtedly she will, she must give more attention to the '*idea*' of the game than in the case of, say, copying the movements of a companion 'tupping along'. Apprehending the pattern of the game becomes at once 'more artificial and more complicated'. . . ."[1]

When the sap rises in the tree, children's senses quicken. But it is when the buds burst open on the branches that their feet grow really light and airy. Of all Nature's rhythms and moods it is the spring-urge that infects children most noticeably.

Daffodils have nodded, and by their movements have seemed to invest human hands and arms with irrepressible miming instincts. The whole pattern of life has become filled with animal urgency, a dance of reawakening, "the leaping of rock unto rock".

Monkey-like, and clutching cords of hemp or tow, they will trapeze through the air. Buck-like, they will vault over railings and the cross-bars of country gates, or frog-jump over each other's backs—like the grasshoppers in the old community camp-song.

April ushers in the legato-movement of the seesaw, the measured or accelerated delight of swinging (31, 32). Yet above anything, is this month consecrated to ropes. Its emblem you might aptly design as a rope uncoiling into the fiesta of swinging and the craze of skipping.

Knotted and tightly wound around city lamp-posts (which are the back streets' maypoles), rope-lengths become impromptu chair-a-planes hoisting miniature bodies off the ground and dangling them exultantly in a merry-go-round's aerial frenzy, feet tapping the earth rhythmically at the crest, and hunched in like a waterfowl's at the trough of the hurtling body's wave.

Skipping may continue all summer through, well into autumn, and until the daylight thins earlier; but it is most assuredly in April when the skipping rope is rediscovered and is brought to light.

Strutt says of skipping that "this amusement is probably very ancient". He remarks that "boys often contend for superiority of skill in this game, and he who passes the rope about most times, without interruption, is conqueror. In the hop-season, a hop-stem stripped of its leaves is used instead of a rope, and in my opinion it is preferable. . . ."

[1] Sir Percy Nunn, *Education, Its Data, and First Principles*, p. 139.

In the *Dictionnaire des Antiquités Grecques et Romaines*[1] under the word "Ludi", you will find an illustration. It is of a statue of a Grecian maiden in the act of swinging a rope over her head. There is no doubt that the rope is made from vine-strands.

Perhaps in this link between the vineyards of the ancient world and the hopfields of modern England we can find a clue to its origin and ritualistic import; namely, that the maidens used plaited vine-strands to propitiate, through ceremonial dances, the pagan goddesses who watched over the sprouting of new growth, the genesis of what would serve to provide cause for harvest's festival and plenty's thanksgiving.

Bett would seem to subscribe to this view, for he writes:[2] "Skipping as a girl's game (25) prevails during the Spring months of the year—the months when the seed is springing up . . . both

[1] Edited C. L. Sahernberg and Edmond Saglio, vol. III, p. 1361.
[2] *Games of Children*, p. 55.

skipping and swinging are connected with the dancing and leaping that usually accompanied pagan rituals relating to the growth of crops." (27)

The sensory pleasures derived from skipping or swinging movements (33, 34) are in themselves sufficient reason why year after year children revive these games in springtime. This basic engram-complex, to use Sir Percy Nunn's term, would account for the recurrence of the maypole game on lamp-posts, already mentioned. Disparaging the pedantry which this line of thought encourages, Bett further observes that "it looks unnecessary to seek a recondite origin for anything as simple as a child's swing". "The child," he says, "delights in the swaying action and that is enough, one would think, to account for the device."

Of the Magico-religious Theory there have been many exponents, but few, with the exception of Gomme, have gone to the rhymes associated with Skipping Games for comparative analysis, examination of folklore origins, or merely compilation.

Both Gomme and Northall refer to a rhyme beginning "The wind/and the wind/and the wind/blows high . . ." This most widely spread variant which really belongs to the marriage-ritual category (see JUNE), has been co-opted by skipping devotees, and has come to be regarded as a specific skipping-poem. Each confirms that it is entirely English in origin—as are most of the examples collected and cited in *Traditional Games of England, Scotland and Ireland*.[1]

[1] Vol. II, p. 387 et seq.

It is, therefore, curious that this tune has persisted, and is still most commonly heard in Belfast, whither it must have come from Scotland. Presumably it is of Planter origin (24) and took root in the north-eastern parts of Ireland, since those Skipping Rhymes noted in Ireland, prior to 1916, were almost entirely Anglo-Saxon in character and since there is no textual material extant to show whether any Gaelic parallels of this game-pattern occur.

Mr. Hugh Quinn's MS. Collection[1] of Belfast Street Rhymes includes this version:

The wind and the rain and the wind blew high
The rain comes blattering from the sky
(Anne Jane Murphy) says she'll die
If she doesn't get a fellow with a rolling eye.

She is handsome, she is pretty
She is the flower of Belfast City
She is courting, one, two, three,
Please could you tell me who is he?

(Boy runs into rope)

(Albert Johnson) says he loves her
All the boys are dying for her
He raps at the window and he rings the bell
Saying, "My true lover, are you well?"

Out she comes as white as snow
With rings on her fingers and bells on each toe
And says to Albert with a sigh,
"I'm in love with a fellow with a rolling eye."

The Cork variant has "spattering" as the onamatopœic equivalent of "blattering": you read "Dublin" for "Belfast" in the capital variant, and "marble eye" as an interesting development of "rolling eye", which in its turn is an obvious corruption of "roving eye" in the English originator.

This example is interesting. It has a complete literary sequence. And this is more the exception than the rule. On account of the continuous nature of skipping itself, Skipping Rhymes frequently become tagged on to each other, in order to sustain the

[1] Lent to the writer.

continuity, so that a Skipping Game may be sung to a catalogue resembling in its construction a series of different folktunes set to an orchestral arrangement. Such *enjambement* is a perfectly natural way of filling gaps caused through loss of memory, and of bringing to a necessary conclusion the flux and the basic pattern of the game.

These patterns vary. Lambert,[1] whose researches in France confined themselves to the Children's Games of the Midi, in the 1906 edition of his book on this subject, included only sixteen variants. Gomme, who may be said to have carried out the most extensive survey in the British Isles, lists about eleven—and these mostly from a London source. Rhymes, also limited to London, were later in 1916 published by Norman Douglas,[2] who merely presented an unclassified anthology, with a sardonic preface attacking pedantry, but without any serious annotation. Gomme enumerated the types of game reported, as follows:

Pepper, Salt, Mustard; Rock the Cradle; Chase the Fox; Visiting; Begging; Winding the Clock; Baking Bread and *The Ladder*. Each type is described in detail.

Pepper, Salt, Mustard, Vinegar, etc., is, in Ireland, found throughout the whole country. It is also generally used, together with an extract from the *Tinker, Tailor* formula, which in country parts is the incantation accompanying oracular games aimed at prophesying sweethearts.

[1] *Chansons Populaires.*

[2] *London Street Games.*

In the melting-pot of the generations many of the traditional verses have become unrecognisable. The outlines remain, however, worn and frayed betimes, and it is remarkable just how many of the original words do resist erosion. But it is the nature of street-games that they are continually undergoing organic changes and so new ideas and new expressions are constantly being invented to fill the antique rhythmic moulds.

Appropriately, the majority of these rhymes preserve in the phrasing injunctions to turn or to bend or to double-skip. In the collection of Skipping Rhymes that follows, such actions are indicated by Roman type. The rhymes have all been taken down from the children themselves, during the past few years, and in all parts of the British Islands.

SOME SKIPPING RHYMES

Early in the morning at half-past eight
I heard the postman knocking at the gate
Postman, postman, drop your letter.
Lady, lady, pick it up,
I spy a lark, shining in the dark,
Echo, echo, G.O. stands for GO!

* * *

Early in the morning at eight o'clock
You shall hear the postman's knock,
Post-boy, post-boy, drop your letter,
Lady, lady, pick it up.

* * *

Dancing Dolly had no sense
She bought a fiddle for eighteen pence
But the only tune that she could play
Was "Sally get out of the donkey's way!"

* * *

Salt, pepper, mustard, vinegar, etc.

* * *

Tinker, tailor, soldier, sailor, etc.

* * *

I know a woman
And her name is Miss
And all of a sudden
She goes like—this.

Monday night—the gramophone.
Tuesday night we're all alone.
Wednesday night I call the roll,
Maureen, O Maureen,
Bonny, bonny Maureen,
All the boys and all the girls
They love bonny Maureen.

* * *

There's somebody under the bed
Whoever can it be?
I feel so very ill
I call Bonnie in.
Bonnie lit the candle
Nobody there!
Hi, hi, diddly-ie,
And out goes she!

* * *

As I was in the kitchen
Doing a bit of stitching
In came *a bogy man*
And I walked out.
I saw a lark, shining in the dark.

* * *

Stand at the bar
Smoking a cigar
Laughing at the donkey
Ha—ha—har!

I see the moon and the moon sees me,
God bless the moon and God bless me,
Grace in the garden, grace in the hall,
And the grace of God be on us all.

* * *

Ice-cream, a penny a lump
The more you eat, the more you jump!
Eeper Weeper. Chimney sweeper,
Married a wife and could not keep her.
Married another,
Did not love her,
Up the chimney he did shove her!

* * *

Mrs. Brown lived by the shore,
She had children three and four,
The eldest one is twenty-four
And she got married to the man next door.

One 'brella, two 'brellas, three 'brellas, *etc.*

* * *

House to let,
Apply within,
When you go out,
Somebody else comes in!

* * *

Teddybear, teddybear, touch the ground;
Teddybear, teddybear, turn right around,
Teddybear, teddybear, show your shoe
Teddybear, teddybear, that will do:
Teddybear, teddybear, run upstairs,
Teddybear, teddybear, say your prayers;
Teddybear, teddybear, blow out the light,
Teddybear, teddybear, say good night.

* * *

Round apple, round apple,
As round as can be
She's dying to see
John Murphy, John Murphy,
He's dying to see
Annie Askins, Annie Askins go round:
Up comes her dear father
With knife in his hand
Sez, "Give me your daughter
Or your life I shall have"
Who cares not, who cares not,
For Annie loves me
And I love her.

* * *

Mademoiselle
Went to the well
Combed her hair
And brushed it well,
Then picked up her basket *and* vanished!

* * *

Datesy, datesy,
Miss the rope
Your're out . . . (repeat).

* * *

Up a ladder, down a wall,
A halfpenny loaf will do us all,
A bit for you, a bit for me,
And a bit for all the familee.

Some rhymes accompany a simple pattern, such as *Doctor Long*, *Monday Night*, *I see the Moon*, etc., in which two hold the rope and a single girl skips in time to their incantation. Others, like *All in Together, Girls*, in which two hold the rope and about four or five enter the game together. In the case of *Up a Ladder*, two hold the rope while two skip into it, one skipping around the other in skilful rotation.

31 The "Tandem" Swing

32 The Garden Swing, *circa* 1800

33 A *Louis Quatorze* Swing at Rambouillet

34 In an Eastern City: Swinging to the music of horns

SOME SKIPPING SEQUENCES WITH ACTIONS

O, it's I have the tooth-ache,
A gumboil, a tummy-ache,
A pain on my left side
A pimple on my tongue
A hip, hip hurray!
To be the Queen of May
The Darkie says he'll marry her,
He'll marry her, marry her,
And take her out of the mill.
O we won't go home till morning
Till daybreak does appear . . .[1]

Chanted:
Charlie, Charlie, Chuck, Chuck, Chuck,
Went to bed with two old ducks,
One died, the other cried,
Charlie, Charlie, Chuck, Chuck, Chuck.

Straight into ACTION SKIPPING
Actions:
I am a Girl Guide dressed in blue
These are the actions I must do
Bow to *the King and* bow to *the Queen,*
Stand at ease *and* bend my *knees.*

Straight skipping:
Hie ho! Skippety toe,
Turn the ship *and* away we go
Judy and Jack, dressed in black,
Silver buttons way down her back.

Two in the middle and two at the end,
Each is a sister and each is a friend,
A shilling to save and a penny to spend,
Two in the middle and two at the end.

A most popular game-pattern is one in which a single skipper goes into the rope, singing a rhyme, and, at a selected command, calls in another girl, and immediately vacates the rope: the second girl repeats the process *ad lib.* until the whole line is exhausted.

These orders are concealed in such phraseology as: *In came* a bogy man and *I walked out*; *Fly away*, Peter . . . *Come back*, Peter . . . *Call for me*; *I called Bonnie in* . . . *Out goes she*: Got married to *the man next door*; When *you go out*, somebody else *comes in*; the *Teddybear* sequence is self-evident, and the rhyme beginning "I am a Girl Guide dressed in blue" is of the same class.

The *Eeper Weeper* game consists in two holding the rope and twisting it very low, but not actually tipping the ground. In *House To Let* (p. 64) a single skipper performs to the rhyme and when she is finished, the next jumps in. If in so doing she misses the rope, she is out—and so on.

Another amusing variant is as follows: two players decide to adopt the names of two flowers—one each. They take the two ends of the rope and "twind", i.e. turn it gently at first. Then

[1] Tune of the Key-roll.

each of the waiting players runs in, by turn, makes one skip, meanwhile shouting out the name of a flower. When a player guesses one of the flowers correctly, she takes the end of the rope, replacing the "Flower", who joins in the line.

Skipping is still as widespread as ever it was. O'Casey in his autobiographical description of the streets of Dublin[1] in the last century, mentions skipping as one of the foremost amusements on spring nights:

> Often in the evening when the stars were still pale in the sky, the boys would see the girls skipping at the other end of the street, as many as ten or fifteen of them jumping gracefully over a regularly turned rope. The boys would slink up nearer and nearer to the skipping girls; the girls would occasionally glance disdainfully at the boys, but in their hearts they wished them to come closer. With a defiant shout . . . a boy, bolder than the rest, would jump in merrily; the rest would follow him, and joyous faces of boys and girls would shine out of thin dusty clouds raised out of the road by the skippers' feet dancing in the way of peace. . . .

A corresponding cameo of an English childhood is provided by Alison Uttley[2] in her essay on Games:

> We skipped our way to school along the rough grassy land, through the wood and along the sloping field paths. It was a quick way of getting anywhere, it gave wings to our feet. We skipped in the playground with one big rope which the pupil teachers turned, and forty little and big girls in a long procession danced their way through "Keep the Pot a-boiling". . . .

SKIPPING TIME

All sorts of times are happy times
For little girls like me
Both resting times and romping times
Are always full of glee.

Perhaps the best is reading time,
For reading books like this;
And skipping time—there's skipping time!
Oh! that's a time of bliss.

Observers sufficiently interested in this aspect of the esoteric have commented on how rich in imagination and variety are the street rhymes employed for skipping by the children of Dublin.[3] Numerous such rhymes which I have heard improvised there

[1] *I Knock at the Door.* [2] *Country Things.* [3] Olivia Robertson: *St. Malachy's Court.*

have short staccato quatrains. There is a distinct parallelism between these and certain southern French illustrations given by Lambert in his *Skipping Games of Provence* (26). For example:

Trois petits pâtes!
Ma chemise brûle.
Trois petits pâtes
La voilà brûlée.

or

Ou vas-tu, petit soldat?
—Je pars pour la guerre
Que portes-tu dans t' sac?
—Des pommes de terre.

LITANY RHYMES

Of the Litany-type songs connected with skipping, perhaps the most expressive is that beginning "A rosie apple a lemon or a tart". It is certainly one of the Marriage Games adapted for skipping by the inclusion of a series of questions and answers; for a feature of such is the catechism-structure, which readily lends itself to the phone and anti-phone accompaniment deriving from the Greek chorus.

This game, for all its popularity, fusing so many fragments from other entities into a complete and unified liturgy of play, has not appeared in printed form in its entirety—to my knowledge. That is why there follows here a version of the game, as played nowadays in the town of Tipperary:

Two hold each end of the rope:

A rosy apple, a lemon or a tart,
Tell me the name of your sweetheart,
ABCD EFG HIJ KLMNOP RST UV WXYZ.[1]
Will he marry me?
Yes, no, yes, no, yes, no, etc.
What will you go to the wedding in?
A wheelbarrow, an ass-and-cart,
A side-car, a motor-car, a gig, a hearse?
What kind of dress will you wear?
Silk, satin, cotton, velvet,
Voile, lustre, openwork, rags.
What kind of shoes will you wear?
Clogs, slippers, sandals,
High boots, low boots, button boots, shoes.
What kind of a house will you live in?
Country house, town house, city house, mud house,
Slate house, cement house, thatched house.
How many children will you have?
One, two, three, four, five, etc.[2]
What will he be when he grows up?
A tinker, a tailor, a soldier, a sailor,
A captain, a colonel, a cowboy, a thief,
A Lord, a Prince, a General, a Duke,
A Scotch Highlander . . .
Will he be drunk or sober?
(*If "drunk"*)
Hit him with a poker, a poker, a poker, etc.

(End of game)

[1] At whatever letter the skipper is tripped = initial letter of Christian name. Ditto for surname.

[2] Until skipper stops.

Since old rope costs nothing and can easily be obtained in crowded cities, skipping is a popular pastime among the poor. In courts and alleyways, when school-time is over, there you may see a length of rope lashed to area railings of some old Regency house become a tenement, and now a proscenium for enactments full of miming, poetry and song. You can tune-in to these performances given by juvenile actors for their own entertainment, the onlookers clapping their hands in time as the skippers tap out the endless slip-slap on footpath or flagstones and voices chant in unison those evocative shreds of singsong, like a congregation hymning a lost liturgy, and to which the dancers jump and turn and pirouette. Meanwhile, watch the tense rope flicking the ground with accuracy and cutting the air into the spinning shapes of ellipses.

It seems logical that the locality politics of working-class areas and the social struggles of the under-privileged should have left a deep impress on the city child's folklore—i.e. the street rhymes. In American cities some research has been carried out by interested observers on the literary significance of street-lore—essays and anthologies have appeared in *The New Yorker* and *The New Masses*, to mention but two.[1] But careful fieldwork has yet to be done in such untapped centres as Glasgow, Manchester, Liverpool and Leeds.

In Ireland, especially in the towns, Skipping Games have always embodied sentiments reflecting the independence tradition. During periods of political crisis they became the vehicles for symbolical and cryptic challenge, every bit as potent as the two-meaninged ballads of the Jacobite wars, or of patriotic resistance to invaders the whole world over.

During the period of the Irish Civil War, Dublin children of the city area improvised a variant on this rhyme which has stratified, as effectively as any, those politico-historical values fossilised in the unopened seams of national folklore:

A tinker an' a tailor an'
A soldier an' a sailor, an'
An Auxie-Man, a Black-an-Tan,
An I.R.A. . . . (and so on).

[1] *Vide* also: *The American People*, B. A. Botkin, p. 286 et seq. (songs and rhymes).

35 Chevaux-fondus
Jeux d'Enfants Series, 1850

36 Frog-jump

37 Hop, Skip, and Jump

JUMPING GAMES

38 Leap-frog
After an engraving by Francis Hayman, 1854

39 Vaulting Over Gates
After a painting by W. Collins

40 Girls on a Garden See-saw

41 Dutch boys playing with beam balanced on log

42 "The Exercise of See-saw"
After a painting by Francis Hayman in Vauxhall Gardens, 1862

43 Dancing Around the Village May-pole, May 1st
A Victorian impression of Elizabethan life

Local, as well as national, politics have left a deep mark on the unrecorded folklore of the city child. In Dublin, for example, the case of an eviction during which popular indignation must have run high, perpetuates the name of Duff, in a rhyme the secondary object of which was to rouse any peeler within earshot to furious pursuit!

Harvey Duff, Harvey Duff,
Pay the rent and that's enough . . .

Though the melody, as already noted, is not an essential part of these rhymes, one is intrigued to find that the tune of "God Save Ireland" (cf. "Tramp, the Boys are Marching") and the political implications of local elections at the period it was in vogue still accompanies a Skipping Game, played at Ringsend.

Vote, vote, vote for Connie Whelan,
Here comes the Bobby, at the door,
If you will not let me in,
I will burst the doo-er in,
And you'll never see your Daddy anny more.

The significance of this underlying dread is a good deal more than just the child's average fear of a bogeyman, or its reticence about a policeman.

This one hails from the Kimmage district:

Policeman, policeman, don't take me
I've got a wife and familee
How many children have you got?
Twenty-four—and that's the lot.

Apart from any far-fetched theory that here is a subtle commentary out of the mouths of babes and sucklings on the standards of social justice in a working-class suburb, this verse has still a double interest. It asks a question, "How many?" and it fits faithfully into the metrical system in which the majority of the older rhymes are cast. Thus, in a place where more traditional forms of Skipping Rhymes, such as:

Teddybear, teddybear, touch the ground, or
Cobbler, Cobbler, mend my shoe . . . or
Two little dickybirds sitting on the wall . . . or
I see the moon and the moon sees me

have become completely or temporarily lost, we find a spontaneous reversion to the basic metrical standard line. That is, a quatrain of trochaic lines that scan "tumtiti, tumtiti, tum tum tum". This excites interest because it is the line that goes through Romance literature, right back to the popular line sung by the Roman soldier. Further topical examples are:

1. *Early in the morning at eight o'clock*
2. *Keep the kettle boiling, a-haon, a do, a tré*
3. *I am a Girl Guide dressed in blue*
4. *Up a ladder and down a wall*
5. *Hi, ho, skippety toe.*

School, perhaps, as an association in the unconscious, seems to play a dominant role in the imagery of these rhymes:

Doctor Long is a very good man
He tries to teach us all he can
To read, to write, to spell as well,
January, February, March, etc. . . .
(and so on, down the calendar)

with its more amusing variant:

Doctor Long is a very good man
He tries to teach you all he can,
Writing, reading, 'rith-ma-tick,
But he never forgets to use the stick.

(*b*) *Strawberry, apple, my jamtart,*
Tell me the name of your sweetheart,
A, B, C, D, E, F, G, H, I . . .[1]

Q. & A. *Will he marry me? Yes, no, yes, no, etc.*
Q. *What will you go to the wedding in?*
A. *A coach, a carriage, a wheelbarrow, an ass-and-cart, a side-car, a motor-car, a gig, a horse, etc.*
Q. *What kind of dress will you wear?*
A. *Silk, satin, etc.*
Q. *How many children will you have?*
A. 1, 2, 3, 4, 5, 6, 7, 8, 9, *etc.* (down the numerals).

[1] Down through the alphabet until the initial letter of, first the Christian, and then the surname, is foretold.

(c) *My auld grand-dad made an old shoe,*
How many nails did he put through
1, 2, 3, 4, 5, 6, 7, 8, 9, 10 . . .

Q. *And what is your right age?*
A. (*Seven*) 1, 2, 3, 4, 5, 6, 7.

Notice this obsession with the letters of the alphabet and the numerals; with lists of nouns, litanies of place-names; with the recitation of numbers, and words letter by letter. They are all closely identified with the school life of the child, and lead us to the observations made by Lambert[1] in a footnote to the following Provençal usage. This may offer the correct explanation as to why the counting formula is so recurrent:

Mademoiselle, quel âge avez-vous
Un an, deux ans, trois ans . . . etc.
(Montpellier)

Lambert notes: "C'est un ingénieux moyen, employé dans les classes enfantines, pour apprendre à compter, les plus habilés arrivent parfois jusqu'à cent ans." (26)

"Pour apprendre à compter!" And here in rural areas, where the youthful imagination is every bit as fertile and as rich in improvising rhymes as that of the children in the sunny Languedoc, it seems reasonable to infer (forgetting the memorising tradition of the Irish Hedge Schools) that many a more advanced lesson than the recitation of the numerals has been sugar-coated by the incantations of a Skipping Game; and that into the forefront of the youngster's mind every year, in "the months when the seed is springing up", there also springs up a legacy from Virgil, Ovid,[2] Homer[3] or Callimachus[4]—wound along a piece of rope stretched between little wrists, swung across a pavement, an alley or a country lane:

All in together, girls,
This fine weather, girls,
Get your hat and coat, girls,
Tell your mother you won't be long.

Shoot! Bang! A house on fire!
I spy a lark shining in the dark.
Echo, echo,
G, O, stands for GO!

[1] Vol. 1, Part 3, *La Stateuse*, p. 45.
[2] *Tristia*, III, Eleg. 12 (Hoops, etc.).
[3] *Odyssey*, VI, 99 (Ball).
[4] *Anth. Graec.*, VII, 89 (Tops).

May

The "merrie month" (44) is dedicated to dancing and laughter and traditional maypole sports on the old village greens (43). The greens may be fast disappearing, but the Singing Games and Ring Games survive for those associated with May are mainly on themes of MARRIAGE and COURTSHIP.

MAY-DAY

Hail to the verdant Spring once more!
Hail to the merry month of May!
Behold around the plenteous store
Of garlands and of chaplets gay.

So many little hands employed
In weaving wreaths this festive day;
Delight to them, pure, unalloyed,
To crown their little Queen of May.

NUTS IN MAY (45)

Here we go gathering Nuts in May,
Nuts in May, Nuts in May,
Here we go gathering Nuts in May
On a cold and frosty morning.

Who will you have for Nuts in May,
Nuts in May, Nuts in May,
Who will you have for Nuts in May
On a cold and frosty morning?

We'll have (Tommy) for Nuts in May,
Nuts in May, Nuts in May,
We'll have (Tommy) for Nuts in May,
On a cold and frosty morning.

Who will you have to pull him away,
Pull him away, pull him away,
Who will you have to pull him away
On a cold and frosty morning?

We'll have (Betty) to pull him away,
Pull him away, pull him away,
We'll have (Betty) to pull him away
On a cold and frosty morning.
(Tug of War follows)

"Nuts" in May is really a corruption of "Knots" in May, "Knots" being an old English version of posies, or little knots of flowers.

* * * * *

The light which Gomme sheds on the title appears to be the most revealing of her theories, e.g. a term used by children for "bunches" of may. Bunches of hawthorn were pulled on May Day not only to decorate the maypole, the may "kissing-bush", but also the doors of houses. Lady Wilde mentions may-bushes, around which children in north-east Ireland played their May-Day games, organised country dances, and held courtship revels. But if the term "Knots" was of Anglo-Irish origin, the custom certainly was universal, for Kennedy records great fun-making on the occasion of the may-bush in his native Wexford.

Bett adds a compendium of references to smilar customs in other countries.

For those who wish to find a Græco-Roman origin for the may-bush custom, we need only point to such occasions as the festivals of Thangeles and Pyanopsia, during which boughs or wreaths were borne by singing boys and afterwards hung up at the door of the house.

The two chanting sides, lined up opposite one another, may be a relic of the two families (or tribes!) interested in the forthcoming marriage of their two members. If it is so, then we may assume that "an agreement has taken place" in the course of the singing dialogue.

THE KEYS OF HEAVEN

There stands a lady on the mountain
Who she is I cannot tell
All she wants is gold and silver
All she wants is a nice young man.
Madam, will you walk it?
Madam, will you talk it?
Madam, will you marry me? No!

Not if I buy you the Keys of Heaven,
Not if I buy you a coach and pair,
Not if I buy you a comb of silver
To place in your bonny, bonny hair!
No!

POOR MARY SITS A-WEEPING

Poor Mary sits a-weeping, a-weeping, a-weeping,
Poor Mary sits a-weeping, on a bright summer day.
Pray tell us what you're weeping for, weeping for, weeping for,
Pray tell us what you're weeping for, on a bright summer day.
I'm weeping for my true love, my true love, my true love,
I'm weeping for my true love, on a bright summer day.
Stand up and choose your lover, your lover, your lover,
Stand up and choose your lover, on a bright summer day.

The Wedding Blessing is intoned as follows:

Now you're married I wish you joy,
First a girl and then a boy,
Seven years after, son and daughter,
Pray, young couple, come kiss together.
Kiss her once, kiss her twice,
Kiss her three times over.

ONCE UPON A TIME

"The ancient observances on May Day, the Maypole and garlands, the May Queen, and the chimney-sweeper's pageant, have I fear, passed away throughout the North as well as the South, unless where special pains have been taken by the upper classes to keep up or to revive them. The local custom, now almost extinct, is for the children to carry about dolls, as richly dressed as may be, in baskets of flowers . . . to the Blessed Virgin, patroness of the month of May."[1]

IN AND OUT THE WINDOWS

In and out the windows
In and out the windows
In and out the windows
As you have done before.

Stand and face your lover,
Stand and face your lover,
Stand and face your lover,
As you have done before.

Follow him to London,
Follow him to London,
Follow him to London,
As you have done before.

Kiss her 'ere you leave her,
Kiss her 'ere you leave her,
Kiss her 'ere you leave her,
As you have done before.

THREE DUKES[2]

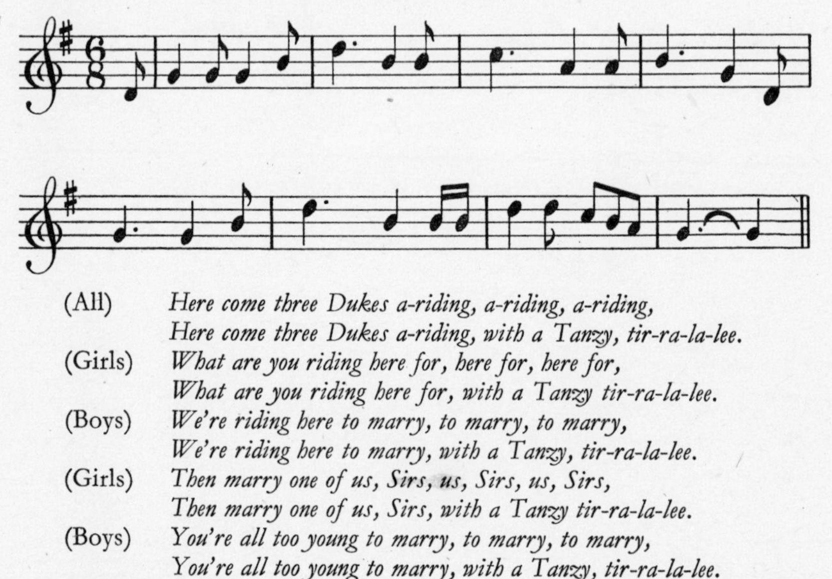

(All) *Here come three Dukes a-riding, a-riding, a-riding,*
Here come three Dukes a-riding, with a Tanzy, tir-ra-la-lee.
(Girls) *What are you riding here for, here for, here for,*
What are you riding here for, with a Tanzy tir-ra-la-lee.
(Boys) *We're riding here to marry, to marry, to marry,*
We're riding here to marry, with a Tanzy, tir-ra-la-lee.
(Girls) *Then marry one of us, Sirs, us, Sirs, us, Sirs,*
Then marry one of us, Sirs, with a Tanzy tir-ra-la-lee.
(Boys) *You're all too young to marry, to marry, to marry,*
You're all too young to marry, with a Tanzy, tir-ra-la-lee.

[1] William Henderson (1879): *Folk-Lore of the Northern Counties of England and the Borders*, p. 85; *vide* also Hone's Works, Vol. I, pp. 271–300.

[2] Current, 1946, Dublin.

(Girls) *We're old enough for you, Sirs, for you, Sirs, for you, Sirs,*
We're old enough for you, Sirs, with a Tanzy, tir-ra-la-lee.
(Boys) *You're all as stiff as pokers, as pokers, as pokers,*
You're all as stiff as pokers, with a Tanzy, tir-ra-la-lee.
(Girls) *We're not as stiff as you, Sirs, as you, Sirs, as you, Sirs,*
We're not as stiff as you, Sirs, with a Tanzy, tir-ra-la-lee.
(Boys) *You're all too black and dirty, black and dirty, black and dirty,*
You're all too black and dirty, with a Tanzy, tir-ra-la-lee.
(Girls) *We're not as black as you, Sirs, as you, Sirs, as you, Sirs,*
We're not as black as you, Sirs, with a Tanzy, tir-ra-la-lee.
(Bowing) *Yet we can bow to you, Sirs, to you, Sirs, to you, Sirs,*
Yet we can bow to you, Sirs, with a Tanzy, tir-ra-la-lee.
(Boys) *Through the kitchen, through the Hall,*
We choose the fairest of you all
The fairest one that I can see
Is pretty Miss (*Sarah*) *come here to me.*

GAMES OF MAYTIME, MARRIAGE AND COURTSHIP

In considering the origin and history of the Ring Game we are led back directly to the fertility cult. *Ring O Rosies* and *Prickly Pear* and *Jingo Ring* are obvious survivors of the pagan rites which were concerned with the propitiation of growth out of primordial earth. The drawing of a crude representation of such a ring-dance exemplifies the ancestry of the modern children's game (p. 146).

We must also note its regional adaptations. Also, that between this and an allied form of the circle idea, namely, *Kiss-in-the-Ring*, there is no great disparity.

Patterns associated with the mythology of marriage and courtship, betrothal customs and superstitions, and wedding ceremonies comprise in themselves a sub-section of Representational Games.

And of *Kiss-in-the-Ring*, Gomme avers with circumspection:

> It is probably a relic of the oldest form of marriage by choice or selection, as compared with marriage by capture. The custom of dropping or sending a glove as a signal of a challenge may have been succeeded by the handkerchief in this game. Halliwell[1] gives the game of "Drop Glove": To throw or fling the handkerchief is a common expression for an expected proposal of marriage which is more of a condescension than a complimentary, or flattering, one to the girl.

Unless we subscribe to the Shavian paradox to the contrary, we might be persuaded that modern marriage is still a matter of free choice on the part of those entering into it. At least, it does smack more of freedom on either side than was, say, the old institution of marriage by capture. Feudal literature makes it very clear just how fully a betrothed woman or a bride was regarded as a chattel, a thing, in the eyes of her spouse, the tribe or the community at large. Bett[2] cites the surviving custom followed by modern grooms who carry their brides across the threshold as a relic of primitive wedding ceremonies.

According to accounts in *The Gentlemen's Magazine* for the years 1767 and 1770, actual bride-capture was practised in Ireland until towards the end of the eighteenth century. Lady Wilde, writing about marriage customs among Ulster folk who were predominantly of Scots-Gaelic descent, tells how a match, no matter how suitable, was regarded as a "lame exploit, even an affront" among the mountainy men, if the groom did not first run away with the bride. Scores of references amplifying marriage by capture describe in detail what used to occur; notably, in the works of Roberts and Brand.

[1] p. 227. [2] *Children's Games*.

In his *Popular Antiquities* relating to an Irish custom, Brand relates how

> the parents and friends of either side, meet on the side of a hill or if the weather is cold, in some place of shelter about midway between both dwellings. If an agreement ensues, they drink the *Agreement Bottle*, as they call it, which is a bottle of good Usquebaugh, and this goes merrily round. Little care is taken for payment of the portion, which is generally a determinate number of cows. . . . On the day of bringing home, the bridegroom and his friends ride out, and meet the bride and her friends at the place of treaty; being come near each other, *the custom was of old to cast short darts at the company that attended the bride*—but at such a distance that seldom any hurt ensued; yet it is not out of memory of man that the Lord Hoath on such an occasion lost an eye: this custom of casting darts is now obsolete. . . . (1682)

This extract *is* of some relevance in showing that marriage by choice or agreement has every bit as old a lineage in Ireland as marriage by capture!

The themes of these Marriage Games all revolve around the idea of matrimony: there are kissing, courting, wooing, wedding, mating, and, of course, jilting themes. A collection of these Singing Games noted down at random follows. With the exception of the first of these, which is quoted from Gomme's collection, they are all still in circulation:

LADY QUEEN ANNE

Lady Queen Anne she sits on a stand[1]
She is fair as a lily, she is white as a swan;
A pair of green gloves all over her hand,
She is the fairest lady in all the land.

Come taste my lily, come smell my rose,
Which of my babies do you choose?
I choose not one, but I choose them all,
So please (Miss Nell) give us the ball.[2]

The ball is ours, it is not yours,
We will go to the woods and gather flowers;
We will get pins to pin our clothes,
You will get nails to nail your shoes, (or, *toes*).

[1] Sedan: i.e. sedan-chair. [2] Ball = posie.

A COLLECTION OF COURTSHIP RHYMES

Apple, jelly, a lemon and a pear
A bunch of violets you shall wear
Gold and silver by your side
Take (Diana Johnston) for your bride,
Take her across the lily-white sea,
Take her across the water,
Give her kisses one, two, three,
She's a lady's daughter.

* * *

I love an apple, I love a pear,
I love a fellow with black curly hair.
O I love him I cannot deny
And I'll marry him, aye, bye and bye.

* * *

Seven o'clock is striking
Mother, may I go out?
My true love is waiting for me without,
I'll wear my beads and ear-rings,
I'll wear my Paisley shawl,
And hand me down my petticoat dress
I'm going to the ball.

* * *

First he bought me apples,
Then he bought me pears,
And then he gave me sixpence
To kiss him on the stairs.
I wouldna take his apples,
I wouldna take his pears,
But I caught him by his wooden leg
And threw him down the stairs.

* * *

Here's an old woman from Sandiland,
Sandiland, Sandiland,
Here's an old woman from Sandiland,
With all her maidens by the hand.
One can knit and the other can sew,
Another can make a dress for a Queen,
So please let her in.

The sweetest maid that I can see
Is (Rosie Kelly), come to me,
Good-bye, Rose, good-bye.

Here's a poor widow who lies alone, lies alone, lies alone,
Here's a poor widow who lies alone,
She wants a man and can't get one.
Choose one, choose, choose the fairest.
The fairest one that I can see
Is (Mary Hamilton) come unto me.
Now she is married and tied in a bag.
She has got a man with a wooden leg.

* * *

There was an old soldier he came from the war,
His age it was sixty and three
Go you old soldier, and choose you a wife,
Choose a good one or else choose none.

* * *

Here's a good widow she lives her lone,
She hasn't a daughter to marry, but one.
Come choose to the east, come choose to the west,
And choose the very one you love the best.
Here's a couple married in joy,
First a girl and then a boy.
Seven years after, and seven years come,
Pray young couple, kiss and have done.

* * *

Off wid the thimble and off wid the ring;
A weddin, a weddin, is goin' to begin.
O Nannie, O Nannie, O Nannie, me joy,
Never be ashamed for to marry a boy!
For I am but a boy and I'll soon be a man,
And I'll earn for my Nannie as soon as I can.
And every evenin' when he comes home,
He takes her for a walk on the Circular Road,
And every little girl that he sees passin' by,
He thinks 'tis his Nannie he has in his eye.

Fused with:

Down in the meadows where the green grass grows,
There's where my Nannie she sounds her horn;
She sound, she sound, she sound so sweet;
Nannie made the puddin' so nice and so sweet.
Johnny took a knife and tasted a bit;
Love, taste; love, taste, and don't say nay,
For next Sunday mornin' is our weddin' day!

Green gravel, green gravel,
Your grass is so green
You're the finest young damsel
That ever was seen,
I washed her, I dressed her,
I robed her in silk,
And I wrote down her name with a glass pen and ink.

All the foregoing examples were being played up to 1947 because I myself took down the words in towns and villages. Note how, often, references to fruit (50) occur in Marriage Games. They are significant clues—symbols high-beached from old fertility rites, withstanding the erosion of the years and are now isolated, like tide-washed juts, without continuity. They are in fact pre-Christian equivalents of such Biblical invocations as *p'ru u'Rvu*, "Be ye fruitful and multiply".

The rhythmic jingle, "A rosy apple, a lemon and a tart", together with its variant "A rosy apple, a lemon and a pear" (both discussed earlier relative to skipping phraseology), has a fascinating history. It is, possibly, one of the few phrases which has a parallel in nearly all the Romance languages—apart from others—with a known corpus of juvenile literature. The phrase has consistently gripped the childish imagination—and stuck hard. In a Dublin back street I came upon the fruit-image personified as an actual personality—a little girl bearing the name of Rosie Apple. (Rosie is a common popular name among Dublin girls.) Rosie evidently became the object of a misadventure on her way to worship—valiantly, on horseback! This is how the celebrant is celebrated in a popular street rhyme:

Rosie Apple went to chapel riding on a pony,
Get two sticks and knock her down and make her stand alone-y.

The version given by Gomme is quite typical of the song as now enacted in Britain:

Rosie apple, lemon or pear,
Bunch of roses she shall wear.
Gold and silver by her side,
I know who will be her bride.

Take her by the lily-white hand,
Lead her to the altar,
Give her kisses, one, two three,
Mrs. (Thompson's) daughter.

You will find this "Rosy Apple" image recurring strangely all through Romance literature. Lambert,[1] in his collection of Tig Rhymes (*formules d'élimination*), including altogether fifty-nine examples, gives these two:

PROVENÇAL

Uno poumo rouge
Que fa le tour de Toulouso;
Uno poumo blanco,
Que fa le tour de Frantso.

FRENCH

Une pomme rouge
Qui fait le tour de Toulouse;
Une pomme blanche,
Qui fait le tour de France.[2]

Une pomme rouge
Qui vient de Toulouse
Simon!
Prenez garde à la maison.
S'il y vient un pauvre
Faites lui l'aumure
S'il y vient un capucin
Donnez-lui un coup de vin![3]

The Old Woman from Sandyland furnishes interesting aspects. Gomme gives nine separate variants, of which a Somersetshire version is:

Here comes the lady-of-the-land
With sons and daughters in her hand.

A Shropshire variant has become "Here comes an old woman from Baby-land". But it is the Gloucestershire variant, most of all, which provides us with a clue to this mythical Sandiland so beloved of Dublin children. There, the opening line of the game runs: "Here comes a poor widow from SANDALAM." Now, it is in the County Down variant that the first marked corruption chronologically takes place. Here it has become "There was an old woman from Sandiland", in which the transliteration of the two words "widow" (into "woman") and "Sand*alam*" (into "Sand*iland*") are both very natural developments. It is suggested

[1] *Chansons Populaires.* [2] Belesta, Ariège. [3] Montpellier.

that this County Down version came directly from Gloucester, and arguments in favour of this opinion follow in the course of the next few pages. From the County Down variant to the one now in vogue in Dublin, there are few radical changes.

It is, moreover, the Belfast variant, as quoted by Gomme, which has yielded more to localisms, for in this the poor widow has become a woman with "a local habitation and a name", in addition to a daughter with a linen-worker's trade:

Here is a poor widow from Sandy Row
With all her children behind her
One can knit and one can sew
And one can make the winder go.
Please take one in.

Now poor Nellie, she is gone,
Without a farthing in her hand,
Nothing but a guinea gold-ring,
Good-bye, Nellie, good-bye.

Between the enactment of the two verses a match has been fixed up.

Hugh Quinn, in his manuscript collection of Belfast Games, records the form it takes as *Three Lords*: "A leader marshals a number of girls against a wall. Three boys, disguised with soot-blackened faces and wearing old bowler hats, approach them, singing:

We are three Lords come out of Spain
That we might coort your daughter Jane.
Leader of girls:
My daughter Jane she is too young
And cannot bear your flattering tongue.
Leader of boys:
Then fare thee well, Oh fare thee well,
We'll go and coort some other girl!
Leader of girls:
Come back, come back! Your coat is white,
And choose the fairest to your sight.
Leader of boys:
The fairest one that we can see
Is (Maggie Moore) come out to me.

Maggie was then taken out and led with due ceremony to the opposite wall where she remained. The three Lords then went through the same performance till all the girls were taken away and the Leader of the Girls was left alone. She resolutely refused to budge, and the three Lords sang (to the air of *Nuts in May*):

Ye dirty wee scut ye wouldn't come in,
Ye wouldn't come in, ye wouldn't come in,
Ye dirty wee scut, ye wouldn't come in
To help us with the dancing.

Yielding to cajolement, she sings, *Come back, come back!* etc. They return and lead her to her companions, singing:

Now we have got the flower of may, the flower of may, the flower of may,
Now we have got the flower of may,
To help us with the dancing!

The game then lapsed into the Hop Polka and the Waltz."

THE GAME OF SILLY OLD MAN

Carleton describes in his *Traits and Legends of the Irish Peasantry* the various games played at a wake in rural Ireland; Larry MacFarland's wake, to be precise. Ninety per cent of these games, significantly, are Marriage Games. And, most in favour, is *Silly Old Man*. The narrator is speaking:

There's another game they call THE SILLY AULD MAN that's played this way. A Ring of the boys and girls is made on the flure—boy and girl about—holding one another by the hands; well and good—a young fellow gets into the middle of the ring as "The Silly Auld Man". There he stands, looking at all the girls, to choose a wife, and in the meantime the youngsters of the ring, sing out:

Here's a Silly Auld Man
That lies all alone
That lies all alone.
He wants a wife
And he can't get none.

When the boys and girls sing this, the Silly Auld Man must choose a wife from some of the colleens belongin to the ring. Havin' made choice of her, he goes into the ring along with her and they all sing out:

Now young couple you're married together
You must obey your father and mother
And love one another like sister and brother
I pray, young couple, you'll kiss together.

Concerning this game, Gomme states:

It seems to be one of the group of marriage games arising from the fact that at any gathering of people for the purpose of a ceremonial, whether a funeral or a festival, it was the custom to form matrimonial alliances. The words (i.e. the final quatrain) are used for Kiss-in-the-Ring Games, and also for some marriage games in which the last player is left without a partner.

Mrs. Lincoln records a Dublin version:

Silly old Maid, she lives alone,
She lives alone, she lives alone (*etc.*)
Wants a husband but can't get one.
So now go round and choose your own (*etc.*)
Choose the very one you love the best.
Now, young couple, you're married forever,
Your father and mother you must obey,
Love one another like sister and brother
And now, young couple, please kiss together.

To continue with the rest of the Marriage Games mentioned by Carleton:[1]

The next play, then, is MARRYING. . . . A buchal[2] puts an old dark coat on him, and if he can borrow a wig from any of the old men in wakehouse, why, well and good, he's the liker his work. This is the Priest: he takes and drives all the young men out of the house, and shuts the door upon them, so that they can't get in till he lets them. He then ranges the girls all beside him, and going to the first, makes her name him she wishes to be her husband; this she does of waise, and the Priest lugs him, shutting the door upon the rest. He then pronounces this marriage service, when the husband smacks her, first—and then, the Priest:

Amo, amas, avourneen,
In nomine gomine,
betwuxt and between,
For hoc erat in votis,
squeeze 'm, please 'em,
omnia vincit amor
With two horns to capiet, nap it
Poluphlasboio, the lasses,
"Quid," says Cleopatra.
"Shid," says Antony
Ragibus et clatibus salemus
stopere windous
Nine months.
Big bottle, and a honeymoon
Almeas poque Dido poque
Roymachree
Hum non fiem viat
Lag rag merry kerry
Parawig and breeches
Hoc manifestibus omnium
Kiss your wife under the nose
Then, seek repose!
'Tis done, says the priest;
Vinculum, Trinculum,
And now you're married.
Amen.

[1] *Traits and Customs.*
[2] Young man.

This remarkable piece of rhythmic nonsense is not doggerel proper. It is merely a naked parody of a church marriage ritual. It is a deliberate caricature and, but for its facetious context, almost a sacreligious one. It reveals a coherent link of verbal echoes, though it has no coherence of either language or literary structure. Yet it boasts, in common with what the Surrealists have formulated into a technique based on the "stream of the unconscious", a dramatic validity, if not a poetic one, in the sense that King Lear's Fool, or any conscious acting-by-the-half-wit, constitutes the stuff of highest histrionic moment.

What is the basis of the mock-marriage benediction? Probably a current popular song. Snippets of it appeared earlier than Carleton's date of publication. It may be found as part of a song by one John O'Keefe (1747–1833):[1]

Amo, amas, I love a lass,
As a cedar tall and slender;
Sweet cowslip's grace
Is her nom'native case,
And she's of the feminine gender.
Rorum, corum, sunt Divorum!
Harum, scarum, Divo!
Tag rag, merry derry, periwig and hatband!
Hic hoc horum Genitivo!

WHITE COCKADE

"Well," says Tom, "the next play is in the military line. You see, the man that leads the sports places them all in their seats, gets from some of the girls a white handkerchief, which he ties around his hat, as you would tie a piece of mourning; he then walks round them two or three times, singing:

'Will you list and come with me, fair maid (three times)
And folly the lad with the white cockade?'

Then he sings this, he takes off his hat and puts it on the head of the girl he likes best, who rises up and puts her arms around him, and then they both go about in the same way singing the same words.

"She then puts the hat on some young man, who gets up and goes round with them, singing as before. He then puts it on the girl he loves best, who after singing and going round in the same manner,

[1] *Oxford Dictionary of Quotations for 1941.*

puts it on another . . . and so on. This is called 'The White Cockade'. When it's all over, i.e. when every young man has pitched upon the girl that he wishes to be his sweetheart, they sit down, and sing songs, and coort, as they did at the marrying. . . ."

Obviously a type of game more suitable for older children!

After this comes THE WEDS OF FORFEITS, or what they call PUTTING AROUND THE BUTTON. Every one gives in a forfeit. The forfeit is held over them and each of them stoops in turn. They are then compelled to command the owner of that forfeit to sing a song—to kiss such and such a girl—or to carry some auld man with his legs about his neck, three times around the house, and this last is always great fun. Or, may be, a young upsetting fellow may be sent to kiss some toothless, slavering auld woman, just to punish him; or if a young woman is in any way saucy, she'll have to kiss some auld withered fellow, his tongue hanging with age half way down his chin, and the tobacco water trickling from each corner of his mouth.

The above may be a slight deviation from the normal way of playing forfeits, but it conforms to the Bergsonian postulate that a ridiculous situation provokes laughter because of its inherent "ugliness". We laugh at automatism, rigidness and ugliness. "Ugliness excites our disgust, as opposed to beauty which excites our admiration."[1] The last game that Carleton gives in this animated sketch is called:

PRIEST OF THE PARISH

One of the boys gets a wig upon himself, goes out upon the floor, places the boys in a row, calls on his man Jack and says to each: "What will you be?" One answers, "I'll be Black Cap"; another Red Cap, and so on. He then says: "The Priest of the Parish has lost his considerin' cap. Some says this, and some says that, but I say—my man Jack!" Man Jack, then, to put it off himself, says: "Is it me, Sir?" "Yes, you, Sir." "You lie, Sir." "Who then, Sir?" "Black Cap!" If Black Cap doesn't then say, "Is't me, Sir?", before the Priest has time to call him, he must put his hand on his ham and get a pelt of the brogue. A boy must be supple with the tongue in it! . . .

On this forceful note of the punitive jest, Carleton ends his description of the pastimes based on Marriage Play which

[1] Bergson: *Le Rire.*

accompany the attendance forgathered at Larry MacFarland's wake.

A SCOTTISH COURTSHIP POEM

Queen Mary, Queen Mary, my age is sixteen
My faither's a fermer on yonder green,
Wi plenty o money tae dress me fu bras,
But nae bonny laddie will tak me awa.

Ae morning I rose an I looked in the glass
Says I tae masel I'm a handsome young lass
Ma hauns by ma side an I gied a ha! ha!
Yet there's nae bonny laddie will tak me awa.

* * * * *

A book devoted to an examination of Basque and Catalan rhymes was published in Spain in 1874.[1] Here we find verses analogous, yet having something more in common with the syllabic stress of popular Italian doggerel than with the southern French rhythm:

Poma Midora
que'n salta de torra
los moras vindran,
t'agoforan,
a to ya mi
Mangours rata
Verten cu d'aqui,
Poma Midora
Poma Midora.

The association of the "ring o' roses—pocket-ful of posies" image with fertility and growth, the connection between "roses" and "apples"—i.e. flowers and fruit, with a bride's embellishments—from these indeed it is not a far cry to the identifying of a damsel with the name of some delicate flower. And few flowers are more virginal than the wild rose of late May hedgerows, nor so suggestive of innocence and liveliness as its coyly opening bud. A preamble like the foregoing introduces more fully, and underlines the poetry in, such a Ring Game as they play to this day in County Armagh. There are three solo parts,

[1] *Jochs de La Infancia* (Catalan) by Fransiso Maspons y Labros.

three players are chosen to fill them. These are: Briar Rosebud herself, the Ugly Fay and Prince Charming. The remainder form a circle round the chosen damsel. They form a Greek chorus chanting accompaniment to the action, thus acclaimed:

Briar Rosebud was a pretty child,
(3 times)
Long, long ago.
She lived up in a lonely tower,
(3 times)
Long, long ago.
(Enter Ugly Fay)
One day there came an Ugly Fay,
(3 times)
Long, long ago.
The Ugly Fay gave her a rose,
Long, long ago.
(Exit Fay)

She pricked her finger with the rose,
Long, long ago.
She fell asleep for a hundred years,
Long, long ago.
The Briars grew thick around the tower,
Long, long ago.
(Ring closes)
Prince Charming came and cut them down,
Long, long ago.
(Prince Charming breaks through the ring)
Briar Rosebud is now a happy bride,
Long, long ago.

Another game, involving a larger cast, dramatises a parade of eligible wives. It commemorates the days when oriental despots and great merchant-potentates sent forth their emissaries—or arrived in person—to choose for themselves a wife from among the daughters of the great houses.

This popular Courtship Game, which is "produced" sometimes with the aid of bits of cloth, old costumes, headgear and make-up, is known as *Three Dukes from Spain*.

The title as well as the litany have undergone many changes and corruptions of text. I have heard the introductory line sung as "Here's the King arriving". The metamorphic process is an interesting one. Gomme quotes no less than twenty-three versions from all over England, and two others from Belfast; also one Dublin version, and one from Waterford, the latter two being slightly different from the English norm. The opening line, "There were three Dukes came out of Spain" quite easily, through obvious verbal deformation, became "There were three Jews". Similarly, "There came three Dukes a-riding" (in Dublin) must have been further misquoted as "Here comes the Duke a-riding"; from this, a further corruption made "Here comes the

8

Duke arriving". Finally, by grafting and localisms, the Duke was promoted to King, so that today we meet the version:

ALL: *Here's the King arriving, 'riving, 'riving,*
Here's the King arriving, Y-O-U.
What are you 'riving here for, here for, here for,
What are you 'riving here for, Y-O-U.
KING: *I'm 'riving here to marry, marry, marry,*
I'm 'riving here to marry, Y-O-U.
ALL: *Marry one of us, Sir, us, Sir, us, Sir,*
Marry one of us, Sir, Y-O-U.
KING: *You're all too black and dirty, dirty, dirty,*
You're all too black and dirty, Y-O-U.
ALL: *We're not as black as you, Sir, you, Sir, you, Sir,*
We're not as black as you, Sir, Y-O-U.
KING: *You're all as stiff as a poker, a poker, a poker,*
You're all as stiff as a poker, Y-O-U.
(Exit King)
ALL: *All round the banister, banister, banister,*
All round the banister, Y-O-U.

Though the King in this version rejects the offers of all and sundry, and the slighted maidens dance away their cares by a ring-song around the staircase of some Georgian hallway which has since become a tenement house, the phrase "arriving" leads us to an origin rich with textual analogy.

In her collection of Italian Singing Rhymes, Elisabetta Oddone includes a Florentine version of a similar game, with its accompanying tuneful melody. The title is *E Arrivato l'Ambasciatore*—"There arrived the Ambassador"! A probable derivation. The illustration (46) shows a dark-skinned figure dressed in exotic silks and satins, bedecked with the gems and ornaments of some Ethiopian potentate, possibly the Great Sultan himself. He is in the act of advancing regally to examine the attributes of likely daughters! We are reminded of the casket scene in *The Merchant of Venice*. May this not possibly be the origin of the line "We're not as black as you, sir", which seems to occur nowhere outside the Dublin variant? Again, the idea of "King", instead of "Duke", from "Spain". In the same ratio as a negro would suggest the remote, the exotic, and the mysterious, the fabulous and the fantastic to an Italian *bimba*, so too would the line "Three

Dukes/Lords/Knights from Spain" represent fantasies of colour and mystery to the mind of the average English child. So would the thought of gipsy. In fact, one of Gomme's variants actually has the line "There came three gipsies out of Spain, A-courting of my daughter Jane". But to the Irish child the land of Spain and its connotations are something more than just a region to which he bids the unwelcome rain begone; it is a land of a friendly power, symbolising a traditional Catholic alliance, the alliance immortalised in ballad and song and story; in Mangan's lyric cry "and Spanish ale shall give you hope, my Dark Rosaleen!"; and the "King of Spain's daughter, who came to visit me all because of my little nut tree" (see p. 159).

Here is a compressed literal translation of the Italian game as played in the streets of Florence to this day, *E Arrivato l'Ambasciatore*:

(Enter Potentate)
The Ambassador has arriven
From his mountains and his valleys,
The Ambassador has arriven
Aiola, aiola, aiola!
(Dialogue Chorus between children and him)
What has the Ambassador come here for, etc.
We want a pretty maiden;
What will you dress her in?
We will dress her in goose-skin.
No, that won't do,
We will dress her in a diamond gown,
Yes, that will do! etc.
(Parade of brides)
Here are the brides who are going to marry
With two hundred rings on their fingers,
A hundred there, a hundred there,
Here are the brides on their way.
(They go off)
They're off to Santa Croce,
(They are at the altar)
Here are the brides who are bound in wedlock
And they bind two or three
(They return home)
Here are the brides who go to their places.

These children's folksongs are mainly narrative. And writing on the evolution of *La Chanson Populaire* in mediæval Europe, Verrier[1] makes the important point that all Celtic popular poetry is narrative rather than lyrical.

This would certainly seem to be true of Scottish and Ulster-Scottish balladry also, in the sense that the tragic courtship folk-song *Binori*, in common with Anglo-Scottish border ballads, is essentially narrative.

There came a prince to be her wooer
On the bonny mill-dams of Binori.

[1] *Le Vers Français*, vol. I, p. 105.

44 Bird-nesting 45 "Here we go gathering knots in May . . ."

46 "Here's the Ambassador Arriving"
From an Italian Illustrated Book of Singing Games

47 "Gira Gira Tondo"
Italian equivalent of Ring o' Roses

48 An Arch Game in the eighteenth century

49 Signs of the Zodiac playing a Ring Game

June

Midsummer Night! The twenty-first of June and the Summer Solstice have had all kinds of superstitions, magical lore and ceremonies connected with them. . . . (49)

Many of those ancient customs relating to FIRE, HOLY WELLS and FOUNTAINS and SACRIFICIAL RITES survive in such forms of children's play as the ARCH GAME.

ORANGES AND LEMONS

(Sung in chorus)

Oranges and lemons
Say the bells of St. Clements;
You owe me five farthings,
Say the bells of St. Martin's;

When will you pay me,
Say the bells of Old Bailey;
When I grow rich,
Say the bells of Shoreditch;
When will that be?
Say the bells of Stepney;
I'm sure I don't know,
Says the Great Bell of Bow.
(Intoned or spoken)
Here comes a candle to light you to bed
AND HERE COMES A CHOPPER TO CHOP OFF YOUR HEAD.
THE LAST, LAST, LAST, LAST MAN'S HEAD.

GAMES RELATING TO ARCHES, FIRE AND WATER

1. ARCHES (48)

Compared with the large range of Ring Games still extant, the Arch Game group has been diminishing most markedly in numbers.

Their basic pattern delineates two opposing teams. In this is reflected the conflict notion. The two chosen leaders, representing the function of spokesmanship—harking back to a feudal age—form an arch with their uplifted arms. On occasion the game-sequence will end with a tug-of-war play. This is expressive of the rivalry, enlivened and cherished, between the two teams. The rivalry also has for an antecedent the ancient differences of headmen.

In this category the games which more generally survive are: *London Bridge*, *Here are the Robbers Passing By*, and *Oranges and Lemons*. All have several variants and subdivisions. They are of decidedly English origin, though the sacrificial lineage is buried in the hazy past. The last-named obviously belongs to London, being one which celebrates the church-bells of the City and their tintinabulations.

Of *London Bridge*, Gomme gives no less than nine versions. One of them, the Belfast version, still in circulation, is as follows:

London Bridge is broken down,
Broken down, broken down,
London Bridge is broken down,
Grand says the little bee.

Stones and lime will build it up,
Build it up, build it up,
Stones and lime will build it up,
Grand says the little bee.

Get a man to watch all night,
Watch all night, watch all night,
Get a man to watch all night,
Grand says the little bee.

Perhaps the man will fall asleep,
Fall asleep, fall asleep,
Perhaps the man will fall asleep,
Grand says the little bee.

Get a dog to watch all night,
Watch all night, watch all night,
Get a dog to watch all night,
Grand says the little bee.

If that dog should run away,
Run away, run away,
If that dog should run away,
Grand says the little bee.

Give that dog a bone to pick,
Bone to pick, bone to pick,
Give that dog a bone to pick,
Grand says the little bee.

Thus, with the exception of four verses omitted from the orthodox English version, there is no major deviation, unless it be the refrain.

There was a wooden bridge built over the Thames at Southwark in 994, and it is to this that the words refer. Later, when the Danes were occupying the city, Ethelred the Unready accepted the offer of an alliance from King Olaf of Norway to defeat them. Olaf's strategy was aimed at ruining the bridge. This he effectively brought off in 1008 by making fast ropes from his ships to the pier-timbers and utilising the force of the tide to pull them down.

In 1196 London's burghers built their first stone bridge. It took twelve years to complete. Four years afterwards it was partially destroyed by fire. In Elizabeth's reign it was restored and, judging from the old maps, in characteristic Tudor style, having nineteen narrow arches.

The melancholy burthen of the song is underlined by the disaster of 1666 when the bridge was consumed by the Great Fire, and again by fire in 1673.

* * * * *

"Grand says the little bee" in place of "My Fair Lady". This is an enigmatic phrase, and recurs as "Gran says the little D" in the Cork variant mentioned by Gomme. The words rather puzzled Gomme, who remarked: "To these there is now no meaning that can be traced, but they help to prove that the rhyme originated from a state of things not understood by modern players."

The Cork variant is as follows:

London bridge is broken down,
Broken down, broken down,
London bridge is broken down,
Grand says the little bee.

Lime and stone would waste away,
Waste away, waste away,
Lime and stone would waste away,
Grand says the little bee.

Build it up with penny loaves,
Penny loaves would be eaten away,
Build it up with silver and gold,
Silver and gold would be stolen away,
Get a man to watch all night,
If the man should fall asleep?
Set a dog to bark all night,
If the dog should meet a bone?
Set a cock to crow all night,
If the cock should meet a hen?
Meet a hen, meet a hen,
If the cock should meet a hen,
Grand says the little bee.

HERE COMES MY LORD DUKE
AND HERE COMES MY LORD JOHN
LET EVERY ONE PASS BY
BUT THE VERY LAST ONE
AND CATCH HIM IF YOU CAN.

50 Bob Cherry

ARCH GAMES

51 "Brö, Brö Brille"
Scandinavian version of *Broken Bridges*

52 Thirteenth century
From a wood engraving

53 Norwegian Children in Scotland: "The one who comes last will be put in a black pot!"

The working out of the continuity in this text is highly imaginative. The theory of building bridges as the origin of this game leaves no gaps to be filled in, and still seems to be the most valid explanation (52). Bett,[1] alternatively, has based his summary of the game upon this theory:

> It has been suggested that the game and the rhyme derived from the collapse of London Bridge in the thirteenth century. That cannot be, however, for the game is mentioned in earlier times, and occurs in many different countries. Naturally the bridge has been differently localised. In England it is always *London Bridge*, as one would expect . . . for that must have been for many generations the most considerable bridge in the whole country. In Scotland, the bridge has no local habitation—the game is merely *Broken Bridges Falling Down*. In New England, U.S.A., it is *Charlestown Bridge*, which was built as recently as 1786. In France, again, it is not localised; it is merely *Le Pont Levis*. Rabelais mentions it as one of Gargantua's games, under the name *Aux ponts chus*, *Fallen Bridges*. In some parts of Germany it is merely *Die Meissner Brücke*. In Aargau it is *d' hollandische Brugg*—a form which has survived among the Germans in the United States. In Danzig it is (again in dialect) *de grone Brock*, "the Green Bridge", being the bridge over the Mottlau by the Green Tower. But in nearly all these forms, the essential parts of the game are preserved—the bridge is falling down, there are suggestions that it should be rebuilt in this way or that, and the climax of the game is the seizure of a captive, who is often a malefactor. . . .

Since this game is international in its popularity, each language celebrating a famous bridge of the respective country, we might have expected to find local Irish place-names (or bridge names), especially at those towns which span the Shannon, Lee, Liffey and Boyne, and which enjoy historical reputations. Such, however, is not the case.

The only respect in which the Irish versions deviate from the general run is through this tantalising phrase, "Grand says the little bee", or "Gran says the little Dee".

If only the word in the Cork variant had been Lee instead of Dee, our clue would have led straight to a solution; but no!

The proper answer to the conundrum is really not so far away as it may seem.

[1] *Games of Children.*

It is commonly agreed that this game is of undisputedly English derivation. This being so, it most likely came to Ireland by way of the North-east plantations. A major section of these settlers, Canon Hume tells us in his *Transactions of the Historical Society of Lancashire and Cheshire*, who were "planted" *circa* 1607, hailed from Warwickshire. Let us therefore glance again at the Warwickshire version of the song under consideration. What do we find?

The refrain is, in actual fact, "Dance over my Lady Lee!" Bett provides us with the missing link. He has mentioned an attempt to connect this name Lee with the noble family of Leigh, whose seat is in Stoneleigh. An ancestor of the family was Sir Thomas Leigh, Lord Mayor of London in 1558. Now, there was a story current among the peasantry on this estate. It tells how, about 1900, the bridge at Stoneleigh Park had one or two human victims immured in the foundations. Bett suggests, that whatever the basis of this fable, "Children playing at this game are unconsciously preserving the memory of a dark rite by which a human being was originally sacrificed to secure the stability of a bridge".

If we apply the lesson of distortion to text due to word-of-mouth circulation, and reckon with the vicissitudes which all traditional fragments undergo, we see clearly that "Gran" or "Grand" is a vowel-corruption of "Dance" (e.g. in the foregoing chapter the Belfast version of "White as a lily and fair as a swan" had been deformed into "white as a wand" owing to the peculiarities of regional phonetics. We can surmise (or claim) that "Says the little Dee" (or "Bee") is similarly a deformation of "My Lady Lee". The phrase, by this linking up, becomes reunited with its source—a localisation of "My Fair Lady". Lady = Ladie = Lady Dee. "Lay dee" may be the origin, in semantics, of "little Dee"!

* * * * *

The Nursery Rhyme of *How Many Miles to Babylon* was, at one stage in its development, shaped into a separate Arch Game. In this guise it took on the new name of *How Many Miles to Barney Bridge*.

Gomme cites this Dublin variant among her descriptive notes on the game as it occurs elsewhere: "Children stand in a half circle, tallest at each end. All clasp hands. The two tallest at one end question those at the other end alternately. At the last line, the two that have been answering hold up their hands to form a bridge and all the others thread through the 'BRIDGE', advancing slowly."

How many miles to Barney Bridge?
Three score and ten.
Will I get there by candle-light?
Yes, and back again.
A curtsey to you, another to you,
And pray fair maids will you let me through?
Through and through will you go for the King's sake,
But take care the last man does not make a mistake.

It would appear that this game has become obsolete nowadays.

A game still more widely in circulation than *London Bridge* is *Hear! The Robbers Passing By*, or *Hark, the Robbers Coming Through*. It follows the traditional pattern of moving towards the last man with the formula "Chip, chop, the last man's head's off", and ending on a tug-of-war.

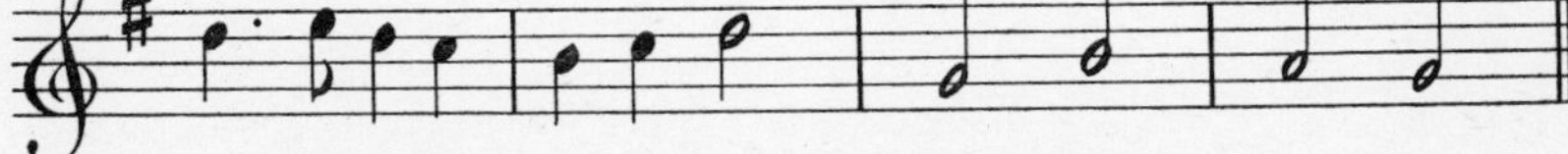

The Dublin version, still in use, and quoted by Gomme:

Here's the robbers passing by, passing by, passing by,
Here's the robbers passing by,
My Fair Lady!
What did the robbers do to you, do to you, do to you?
What did the robbers do to you?
My Fair Lady!
They stole my watch and stole my chain, stole my chain, stole my chain
They stole my watch and stole my chain,
My Fair Lady!

The intoned chorus at the end of each verse, which is accompanied by the chopper actions of the arched arms as they descend like a decapitating pair of axes on the marching players' heads, assuredly enshrines something of the ancient sacrificial killing. The words are:

Chip Chop
Chip Chop
The-last-man's-head-is-OFF!

In vivid contradistinction to the innocuous pastoral ring of the Norfolk localisation ("So round the meadows we must go"), a Belfast variant has for the final line: "Then they all must go to jail" (etc.).

This is the only Arch Game which seems to have outlived a tendency in rural areas towards urbanisation. The melody has exercised a strong appeal on children. It has no traditional equivalent in Gaelic, but an attempt by a schoolmistress has been made to superimpose it on the repertoire of a Claddagh (County Galway) school. This is the one case which I have found, of a *synthetic-Gaelic* game that has had any notable response among children, when introduced from outside by an adult.

As popular as *London Bridge* in England is its Scandinavian counterpart *Brö, Brö, Brille*. In a Danish folklore journal, edited by S. Tvermose Thyregod, an authority on Singing Games, we find a traditional version, duly illustrated (51). It was a matter of interest for me to compare this with the similar version of the Song which refugee children from Norway were playing in a field at Buckie, in North Aberdeenshire (53), when I visited a colony of Norwegian fishermen settled there during the war.

The photograph (53) shows the fisherfolk's children enjoying their game of *Brö, Brö, Brille*.

FROM A TEACHER'S TEXT[1]

RABBIT TRAPS

Half the class stand in pairs round the yard forming a double ring and facing their partners. They join both hands and hold them up to form a "Rabbit Trap". The other half, "the Rabbits",

[1] Noted in 1946.

run round the ring passing through all the traps. When the whistle blows the traps shut, the children lower their hands and try to catch one of the rabbits. If a rabbit is caught in a trap, he changes places with one of the children who forms the trap, and the game proceeds.

2. GAMES RELATING TO FIRE

Obviously, the practice of maintaining a perpetual fire as a part of a religious ritual connects with the early necessity of keeping a fire always alight for the use of the tribe, as does also the practice of rekindling such fires, if they do go out, by the most primitive means, even when better methods have long been familiar. Thus there is a provision in the Law of Moses that "fire shall be kept burning upon the altar continuously: it shall not go out". . . .[1]

HENRY BETT

[1] *Origin of Games*, p. 74.

LONDON'S BURNING
(A Part Song)

London's burning (1st voice) while the next follows:
Come quickly (1st voice)
Fire, fire,
Pour on water, pour on water.[1]

An Ulster Ring Game, accompanied by a refrain, in which the players begin to chase each other, while keeping intact the cyclic formation, is as follows:

Fire on the mountain!
Run, boys, run!
You with the red coat,
Follow with the gun!
The gun shall go, and you shall run.
Fire!

[1] "London's Burning" technically is called a canon, i.e. a melody which, after a few beats, is copied strictly by another part (or voice). One of the earliest canons known is "Sumer is icumen in" (thirteenth century). Canonic writing after this reached every imaginable device.

Bach uses the canon a great deal and with unsurpassing contrapuntal musicality. A fine modern example is the last movement of the Franck Sonata for violin and piano. A. R.

AN ANCIENT HYMN

Sally, go round the sun,
Sally, go round the moon,
Sally, go round the chimney-pots
On a Saturday afternoon.

In an issue of *Irisleabhar na Gaedhilige* appears the following:

"*TROM! trom, cad ta os do chionn?* This is a trick which children of Ballyvourney, West Cork, play. They put a sliver of wood into the fire, and leave it there until it is red; then they take it out. If it is lighting, they put out the flame, so that it has only a glowing end. Then the player who is holding it says to his neighbour: 'Here is my little spit [i.e. fire-spit] for you.' 'What is your little spit worth?' says the other. The first one:

'A live spit, a dead spit,
If my spit dies between your hands
The forfeit will be on you,
A chicken walking the marsh,
Her leg broken and a burden on her.'

When he has said that, he passes it on, and the trick is repeated. It goes round, perhaps three or four times, the speed increasing as the spark dies. Finally, it dies in somebody's hands and then he has to pay forfeit; that is, he has to put a bandage on his eyes, put his head on the seat of a chair, and remain kneeling while the others seek things to place on his back. Suppose the first thing is a sod of turf. They put that on him and say: 'Forfeit, what's on top of you?' He judges it by its weight and says perhaps 'Bottle!' They reply: 'Stay there, sod of turf, till the bottle comes.' Then, another object is put upon his back, and so on until he guesses aright. Then he is released and the game begins again." (Translated from the Gaelic.)

Another variant occurs in the magazine *An Locrann*[1] in the form of an article by Sigle ni Louacain, who claims to have played this game. She is of the opinion that the game is confined to little girls from the phrase:

Sicín circe ag siubal na muinge
Cos di brisce is brat uirthe,

which is supposed to mean "a chicken or hen walking (either) on her breast (or on a morass), a broken leg and a parcel on her, which would describe a girl who would be blindfolded"; but such, of course, is not the case.

Now there is an exact parallel to this game in France, where the formula is "The little gentleman is still alive", and, as Gomme[2] shows, this includes in the relationship the English game of *Jack's Alive*. In Scotland, on the other hand, a rigid superstition attaches to the game. There it is called *Preest Cat*. The myth goes that when the priest's cat departed this life, wailing began throughout the countryside, as people thought it became some supernatural thing, like a witch—so that to keep it alive was a matter of great moment.

Gomme, in another work,[3] comments: "This is a very significant game, and its similarity, in miniature, to the custom of carrying the fiery cross to rouse the clans, at once suggests its possible origin. The detention of the fiery cross through neglect, or other impediment, was regarded with much dread by inhabitants of the place in which it should occur. . . ." This explanation might be acceptable were the game confined to the Gaelic nations; but it is not. We have noted that it occurs in France. According to Grimm,[4] it also occurs in Germany: there, the formula is "If the fox dies, I get the skin", evocative of the conditional mood involved in the penalty or forfeit pattern. This "Forfeit" element gives an added argument in favour of the primitive fire-making character of the game. "There can not be much doubt," writes Bett, "that this is a memory of those early days when fire would be carried from hut to hut, or, in some cases, from tribe to tribe, by means of a burning brand, and when it was quite a serious mishap to let it die out."

[1] *Nodlaig*, 1910, p. 4, col. 3.
[2] *Traditional Games*, vol. I, p. 257.
[3] *Primitive Folkmoots*, p. 279.
[4] *Teutonic Mythology*, vol. II, p. 853.

Though in the Gaeltacht version the glowing stick is a *cipin*, in the English equivalent it is, curiously enough, personified. The name assumed, like so many of the proper names used for the common personages in English folklorist terms of reference, is "Jack". Jack Horner, Jack o' Lantern, Jack Frost, Jack-in-the-Green, and Jack o' Lent, being among the most generally known. This is Gomme's description of *Jack's Alive*: "A number of people sit in a row, or on two chairs around a parlour; a lighted wooden spill or taper is handed to the first, who says:

"*Jack's alive and likely to live,*
If he dies in your hand, you've a forfeit to give."

The Derbyshire version runs:

Leader: *Little Nannie Cockershaw*
What if I should let her fa'?
All: *Nine sticks and nine stones*
Shall be laid on thy bare bones
If thou shouldst let her fa',
Little Nannie Cockershaw.

The forfeit idea as implied here is rare in an English equivalent, and the mention of a specific number of blows to constitute the penalty, even more unusual. If we wished to pursue the line of deduction offered by this English analogy, it might point to an Anglo-Norman ancestry of this game as still played in Gaelic-speaking Ireland only.

Gomme quotes another game with the name of *Dan'l my Man*:

A little slip of wood or straw is lit and blown out, and while it is red it is passed round from one to another, each one repeating as fast as he can:

Dan'l my man,
If ye die in my han'
The straddle and the mat
Is sure to go on.

The player in whose hand the spark dies has to go down on his knees. A chair (or some other article) is put over him and he has to guess what it is, while the others cry out: "Trom, trom, what's over your head?" If he is wrong, it is left on him, and another article brought along.[1]

[1] Kiltubbrid, County Leitrim.

We find an apposite reference to a similar game in the fifteenth century. It is mentioned in Rabelais as "Foucquet". An editor of Rabelaisian glosses gives its origin as "Foulque"—a little squirrel. They called the game *Little Squirrel*, which in Anjou consists in trying to "put out" a lighted taper with their noses, no doubt because of the rich fire-red hue of the squirrel's coat—another case of totemisation of the fire concept.

The sacrosanct properties of fire are further commemorated in a game, once played in Cork, and now obsolete. The following version, coming from the pen of Miss Keane, is called *Fire, Air and Water*:

> The players seat themselves in a circle. One of them has a ball to which a string is fastened, so that he may easily draw the ball back again, after it is thrown. The possessor of the ball then throws it to one in the circle, calling out the name of either of the elements he pleases. This player must, before ten can be counted, give the name of an inhabitant of that element. When "Fire" is called, *strict silence must be observed, or a forfeit paid.*

3. GAMES RELATING TO WATER AND RAIN

George Lawrence Gomme, writing in 1892 on the ethnological aspect of well-worship, pointed out that:

> . . . the cult is so general in Ireland that it has not received the attention of Irish antiquaries that it deserves . . . the ceremonies of well-worship in Ireland present practically the same features, though in a far more intensified form, than those in Wales. The processions round the well, sunwise, are an important and nearly universal part of the ceremony, which the Irish evidence introduces into the subject. . . . Besides restoring the unimportant details of Welsh ritual to an important place in well-worship, Irish evidence introduces an entirely new feature. . . .

Irish evidence introduces an entirely new feature. Having stressed this point, the author next cites various localities in Ireland in which the cult was still surviving at the time of writing his treatise. From his observations we find that the cult of the Rain God appears in the example recorded at Innismurray Island, off the Sligo coast.

The cult of the Rain God has given rise to the odd fragments of rhymes, charms, saws, runes and proverbs which constitute the branch of folklore better known as Weather-wisdom. When met with today, they invariably point to common-sense observation about storms, rains or drought. In pre-Christian times, however, weather magic was a vital part of sacred lore; it was the prerogative of the oracles, or the elders. It was also a weapon in the hands of the wizards of the community.

It may be that the childhood jingle originates in some such prayer created in that remote age:

Rain, rain, go to Spain,
And never come back again.

An interesting parallel with this verse exists in the literature of ancient Greece. There is an Athenian prayer quoted by Marcus Aurelius that goes:

Rain, please dear Zeus, send rain
Over the fields, to Athens
And over the fields of the plain.

Here, the mood of invocation is a conscious adult appeal to some supernatural power. It is a serious matter. Especially in the countries of the East where irrigation, and consequently the harvest and bread, the staff of life, depended upon generous rains. Part of the Jewish liturgy for the Festival of Passover still retains a long poetic Litany for Rain—a relic of the pastoral life led by the Hebrew nation in the Holy Land. But, for the child, rain has a totally different connotation. The child prays for its cessation and does not evoke a surfeit of it. Regarded as a disaster, identified with disappointment, the rain is something inexorable which calls a halt to outdoor activity, cancels a promised picnic or keeps him, a temporary prisoner, behind drop-pattering window-panes. Picture the children of ancient Greece; whenever a cloud passed over the sun they would clap their hands and sing out:

Shine out, my dear Sun.

They called it the Sun Game, but it must have been less a game than an incantation, learned from their elders, and imitated.

An interesting fragment is the opening singsong occurring as an introduction to the *Wallflowers* games played in parts of northern England:

> *It's raining, it's raining, it's raining on the rocks,*
> *All the little fisher girls are handing out their frocks.*

From such quotations as the foregoing, Lawrence Gomme deduced the ethnological formula.

In investigating such, we soon realise that the acts of simple reverence, garland-dressing and the dedication of a well to a Christian saint (this last, a most recent expression in popular folk-tradition) are direct developments of primitive acts: ". . . On Welsh ground, the highest point of primitive culture is the tradition of the animal guardian spirit; (whereas) on the Irish ground, it is the identification of the deity with the rain-god. . . ."

More actual references are found in a work by W. Y. Evans-Wents, who, after having made a profound study of *The Fairy Faith in Celtic Countries*, states:

> In these cults of sacred waters, numerous non-Celtic parallels could easily be offered, but they seem unnecessary with Celtic evidence so clear. And this evidence which is already set forth, shows that the origin of worship paid to sacred wells, fountains, lakes or rivers, is to be found in the religious practices of the Celts, before they became Christianised.

Commenting on the theistic beliefs of these Celts, Canon Mahé[1] puts the matter thus:

> The Celts recognised a supreme God, the principle of all things; but they rendered religious worship to the genii or secondary deities, who, according to them, united themselves to different objects in nature, and made them by such union, divine. Among the objects were rivers, the sea, lakes, fountains. . . .

More reliable research in the field of anthropology and of Irish archæology has produced evidence, congruent with that furnished by American workers, to the effect that the "Teutonic-versus-Brythonic Celt" theory has little foundation.

What G. L. Gomme[2] did establish, nevertheless, has not been

[1] *Essai*, p. 323.
[2] *Ethnology of Folklore.*

refuted by subsequent scientific investigation. This is the theory that two distinct cultures existed contemporaneously in England from far fore-Celtic times, and whether we agree to call them "Upland" and "Lowland" cultures instead of the convenient designations assigned by those earlier scholars, or by any other equally descriptive terms, they do represent one line of culture which is pre-Celtic in origin. From some sources, games of Asiatic and Nile Valley origin have reached Irish shores independently of British agencies. Another line of culture has deflected and permeated throughout the different invasion-influxes and Planter-strains in a manner which is elsewhere discussed (p. 98).

Wallflowers, as Saintyves has shown in *Les Liturgies Populaires*,[1] is a relic of those circumambulatory incantations in the presence of sacred wells and fountains.

[1] p. 19.

Gomme actually cites thirty-five different versions of the game. There is one included from Howth, County Dublin, as follows:

Wallflowers, wallflowers, growin' up so high,
Neither me nor my baby shall ever wish to die,
Especially (——), she's the prettiest flower,
She can dance and she can sing and she can tell the hour,
With her wee-waw, wee-waw, turn her face to the wall.

The final line in the Waterford variant is: "Turn your back to the game."

The Belfast version[1] is as follows:

Mary Kelly's stole away, stole away, stole away,
Mary Kelly's stole away and lost her lily-white flowers.
It's well seen by her pale face, her pale face, her pale face,
It's well seen by her pale face, she may turn her face to the wall.

The implication of her being a changeling child, her face being a translation due to faery intervention, is an interesting sidelight, occurring as it does in a County Antrim region.

In his scanty chapter devoted to "Les rondes auprès de l'eau" Saintyves clings tenaciously to his theory that dances performed near wells and streams and fountains are survivals of well-worship: "Les filles ont toujours eu en rôle préponderant dans la ronde, sans doute en souvenir du rôle des muses, des nymphes et des dryades, dans les cultes païens. . . ."

Bett accepts unequivocally the same conclusions. Neither of these students has attempted to answer the question whether, in France at any rate, the war of the Church against water-cults, and the magic that was centripetal to them, had not more than partly succeeded in quelling the tendency, and that by the beginning of the thirteenth century these "danses" and "rondes", consecrated to pre-Christian well-worship, had been by-passed into canals of folksong—what in France they call "Chanson Populaire".

Verrier's monumental work on metrics[2] contains a series of first-line examples from texts of "chansons populaires" which certainly seem to point to an argument in favour of this view. For example, in his chapter on twelfth-century and thirteenth-century *caroles*, he includes several songs for metrical analysis. He is not

[1] Hugh Quinn's MSS. [2] *Le Vers Français*, vol. II.

concerned with facts outside their textual history and their technical anatomy: from their complicated rhyming schemes and the subtlety of their musical structure they would seem by then to have grown into that original and sophisticated repertoire of the *trouvères*.

Yet numbers of these *caroles* are about fountains: they are about events, crises, love-affairs and adventures that invariably open up to an essential choreography of river, fountain, or the sea itself.

So many Singing Rhymes are addressed to Sally. It is probable that she is an English derivation from "Sulis". Sulis Minerva was a Roman presiding water-deity.

"Little Sally Waters" is most certainly the same personality.

SALLY WATER

Sally, Sally Water,
Sprinkle in the pan,
Rise, Sally, rise, Sally,
And choose a young man.
Bow to the East
And bow to the West,
And bow to the pretty maid
That you love best.

My Lady's Daughter, sometimes called "Draw a Pail of Water", is another such fragment. Haliwell, in *Nursery Rhymes*, describes the action thus: "A string of children, hand in hand, stand in a row. A child stands in front of them as leader; two other children form an ARCH, each holding both the hands of the other. The string of children pass under the arch, the last of whom is taken captive by the two holding hands. The verses are repeated until all are taken."

The words, according to Gomme, refer firstly to drawing water from a sacred well, and secondly to collecting flowers for dressing the well.

Victorian picture-books illustrated the theme literally, and not the actions of the game.

MY LADY'S DAUGHTER

Draw a pail of water
For my Lady's daughter.
Father's a King,
Mother's a Queen,
My two little sisters are dressed in green,
Stamping marigolds and parsley.

July

With Nature and growth at the zenith, most of play-time is now spent in the open air (57), where wild life provides the natural themes for games connected with BIRDS, FLOWERS (55), INSECTS (58) and ANIMALS.

THE RING O' ROSES

A ring, a ring o' roses,
A pocket full of posies,
A-tisha, a-tisha!
We all fall down!

FLOWERS, BEASTS AND INSECTS

A fondness for flowers and for growing plants evokes an instinctive love and admiration among small children. Long before Nature Study became a school subject, the vocabularies in their games, in scores of languages, were as comprehensive as many a note-book.

Watching a child clutch out to tip the growing flower from earliest childhood, suggests a deep instinct for the beautiful. Beneath the literary structure of the games themselves we may discover a substantial skeleton-work of pagan fertility prayers.

We have noticed, for one thing, how roses, bluebells, lilies and wallflowers feature in the imagery of impromptu and spontaneous street-play. We have commented, in particular, on the persistence of the wallflower image, though its verbal ancestor was unmistakably "Water". We have come across, worked into the incongruous jingles, the Skipping Games, the generality of oranges and lemons, apples and pears, strawberries, peaches and plums. Likewise we could pursue a liberal recurrence of tree-references in games involving circumambulation; to willows, salleys, rose-bushes, the nut-tree, mulberry bush, prickly-pear, and so on. Finally, we have observed how the rustic festival of

May Day with its custom of the may-bush, has a folklore and a mythology entirely its own.

It was with the festival of Maytime that an interest in flowers really begins—from the aspect of folk-custom. An old woman, in the County Wexford to whom I was chatting in 1940—she was over eighty then—reminisced:

> We'd cut down a branch of may tree and put it in an empty tub, and then decorate it with coloured papers and silk ribbons. Then each one of us would bring a candle, and place it, lighting, on the bush. We had games and singing around the bush, until all candles were burnt out. All children from anywhere nearby, were welcome. We had sugarsticks and gingerbreads and biscuits.

Schoolchildren, according to this lady, played a most artistic game during the spring and summer seasons. It was called *The Penny Peepshow*. Each child would collect bright petals and leaves and ferns: bits of geranium and wild flowers together. They would be arranged in a personal design upon a base of cardboard, pressed down and bound with an equal-sized plate of glass. During play-hour a brisk traffic would ensue among the peep-showmen who displayed real artistic skill, and competed freely to win custom. Since there was a fee charged to enjoy these kaleidoscopic works of floral art, the advertising slogan, "Penny to see the peepshow", loudly chanted, was a natural prelude to the viewing. And remarkable now to us (familiar with the wonders of sixpence worth of the cinematograph's magic) is the fact that the youthful customers considered the exhibitions of patient workmanship and individual artistry well worth the charge. "Penny to see the Grotto" is a similar amusement (70).

Addressing growing flowers with snatches of incantations or verse, is another form of play which has an ancient history. Common to the children of many countries, the pulling off of petals has oracular significance. In England the flower most generally connected with this practice is the ox-eye daisy, or "dog-daisy". As the petals are torn off, one by one, each child chants alternatingly the pronouncement that its beloved is true, and that its beloved is not true. On the last surviving petal hangs the final truth.

54 Flowers for making Daisy Chains
A Kate Greenaway drawing

55 From an Edwardian picture-book

56 "What time is it . . . ?"

57 Picking Posies and Climbing Trees

GAMES WITH FLOWERS

58 Butterfly Catching, 1344 (*Roman d'Alexandre*)

59 "Here we are on Tom Tickler's ground"

60 "Ladybird, Ladybird . . ."
From a late-Victorian toy-book

A similar game is played with the fluffy heads of the common dandelion in full seed, sometimes known colloquially as "clocks". The time of day, hour and minute, are in this way divined. The child blows upon the winged gossamer-like seeds, exclaiming the numbers on the clockface between each blow. When the seeds are all launched on the breeze, and the bare receptacle remains, the correct time (according to fairy calculations?) is ascertained.

Here are the formulæ used in Oracle Games:

1. With the petals of dog-daisies:

   He (she) loves me,
   He (she) loves me not! . . . ad lib.

2. With the puffy seeds of dandelions (56):

   What time is it?
   One o'clock (blowing on seeds),
   Two o'clock . . . (*ad lib.* round the clock).

   Daisy Chains (54).

3. With Buttercups:

   Do you like butter? (Tickles chin with petals.)
   (If the other child smiles) *YES!*
   (If not) *NO!*

TOM TICKLER

Here we are on Tom Tickler's ground, (59)
Picking up gold and silver!
'Mong daisies and lilies
And daffadowndillies.
Oh, who wouldn't be a delver?

TWO LITTLE DICKIE-BIRDS

(A game played with paper wings on fingers.)

Two little dickie-birds sitting on a wall,
One called Peter, the other called Paul,
Fly away (actions) *Peter; fly away, Paul,*
Come back (actions) *Peter; come back, Paul!*

TWO ANCIENT INSECT CHARMS

SNAIL, SNAIL

Snail, snail, put out your horns.
And I'll give you bread and barley-corns.

LADYBIRD, LADYBIRD

Ladybird, Ladybird, fly away home, (60)
Your house is on fire and your children are gone
All except one who lies under a stone,
Ladybird, Ladybird, fly away home.

In the south of France, where there are such gaudy varieties, *Talking to Insects* is another form of amusement. Apart altogether from the curiosity of little boys whom a latent sadistic urge drives to pull the limbs and wings from off "Daddy-long-legs", or the phobia that associates the harmless spider with ambush—through the Miss Muffet rhyme—a butterfly's painted lure, or a dragonfly's mauve lustre, must exercise a powerful fascination for youngsters walking in a meadow or along a woodland path, having not a care for anything but the weather.

From earliest times, certain insects were associated with the movement of the sun, among them the ladybird. The Egyptians held the chafer (khefer) sacred, and the ball it rolled along, containing its eggs, was identified with the solar orb. The khefer was esteemed as the beneficent power that helped to keep it moving.

Chafers that had the power of flight were peculiarly sacred. Indian legend tells how the ladybird (Indragopas) flew too near the sun, singed its wings and fell back to the earth.

Ladybird rhymes embody the idea of divination. The most popular of these invokes the insect to return to its house which is in danger of being destroyed by fire, and its children being lost if it fails to return. It appeared in a nursery collection as early as 1744 (see p. 116).

In local variants the insect is addressed by country names. Some of these are: Lady Cow, Gowdenbug, Dowdy Cow, Burnie Bee, Bishop-Bishop-Barnabee.

Montgomerie in his *Scottish Nursery Rhymes*[1] includes a variant in which the insect is called a Laundress, since the Mother Divinities were also credited with the patronage of rain, weather and (therefore) washing:

Leddy Leddy Landers
Leddy Leddy Landers
Take up yer coats aboot yer haid
And flee awa tae Flanders.[2]

And in a Kincardineshire collection of 1892 we find another interesting variant:

King, King Golloway,
Up your wings and fly away
Over land and over sea
Tell me where my true love can be.

* * * * *

Lady-Cow, Lady-Cow,
Fly away home!
Thy house is on fire,
Thy children are flown,
All but a little one
Under a stone,
Fly thee home, Lady-Cow,
'Ere it be gone.

Foreign parallels of these rhymes are numerous. In Switzerland they sing:

Goldchäber, flüg uf, uf dine hoche Tanne,
Zue diner Muetter Anne.
Sie git dir Chäs und Brod.
's isch besser as der bitter Tod.

[1] page 30.

[2] Quoted in full, p. 31, by Robert Ford (*Children's Rhymes*, 1904).

A charming myth surrounds the ladybird's assistance to the Virgin Mary, who had lost her keys of heaven. It is known as "The Lady Mary's Key-bearer" in Sweden and parallels repeat the theme of love divination, for example, this Swedish rhyme:

Jungfru Marias Nyckelpiga,
Flyg ëster, flyg vester,
Flyg dit der bor din älskade.

Whereas the German are quite as variated as their English counterparts. Thus, an Insect Rhyme sung in Saxony:

Himmelsküchlein, flieg aus!
Dein Haus brennt,
Deine Kinder weinen alle miteinander,

contrasts with the Potsdam rhyme:

Marienwormken flig furt
Flig furt nach Engelland!
Engelland ist zugeschlossen,
Schlüssel davon abgebrochen.

Ladybird (lit. *Mary's insect*), *fly away,*
Fly away to Angel-land,
Angel-land is locked, the key is broken off.

The enjoyment felt by children in addressing insects extends likewise to spiders, grasshoppers, daddy-long-legs and, of course, snails and bees.

Bless you, bless you, bonnie bee,
Say when will your wedding be.
If it be tomorrow day
Take your wings and fly away.

* * *

Snail, snail, shoot out your horn
And tell me if it will be a bonny day the morn.

So close to the French parallel is our rhyme expressing the invocation to the snail, that one might contend that it is a literal adaptation from it:

Snail, snail,
Put out your horns,
Your house is on fire
And your children are gone!

This is, in fact, a variant of the little poem that is addressed to any ladybird which happens to alight upon the child, or anything close to it:

Ladybird, ladybird,
Fly away home,
Your house is on fire
And your children are burned!

The rhythm is, of course, in the beat of the popular trochaic, as borrowed from the nursery, e.g. "Pussycat, pussycat, where have you been?", "Teddybear, teddybear", etc., "Dickybird, dickybird", etc.

SONG TO A DRAGONFLY
(An old Dialect Rhyme)

Snakestanger, snakestanger, vlee aal about the brooks;
Sting all the bad bwoys that vor the vish looks
But let the good bwoys ketch aal the vish they can,
And car'm away whooam to vry 'em in a pan;
Bread and butter they shall yeat at zupper wi' their vish
While aal the littull bad bwoys shall only lick the dish.

The custom of talking to birds may have its roots in some primordial fetish, but for our purposes we must content ourselves with the fact that the instinct is still paramount.

Talking to animals is a custom more easily tracked down. In Gaelic literature there are several instances of charms and runes addressed to cattle. And oxen, wheresoever they are used, are coaxed and encouraged to labour by song.

Milch cows are induced to yield their milk in the same way. Such is the Scottish folksong—one of the most lovely of the milkmaids' ditties—as mentioned by Maclagan in the *Folklore Journal*:

Cush-a-cow bonny, come let down your milk,
And I will give you a gown of silk,
A gown of silk and a silver tee
If you will let down your milk for me.

With regard to an innate healthy element of cruelty, or even a more morbid tendency towards unconscious sadism, it must be accepted, with Nunn's conclusions in general, and the hormo-mnemic theory in particular, that children undergo a phase of aggressiveness which may anticipate, in childhood, the role of attack which they may be called on to fill in adult life; in which case, the origin of this psychosis in the memory of the race may go back to an era when savageries were a commonplace.

It is apt, also, to remember that for popular amusement the Romans laid stress on the side of the Arena Games. Those spectacles which aroused most pleasure under the ægis of war-like and imperial-minded Rome, were the sight (regarded as quite normal) of unequally matched animals tearing each other to pieces and the contest of man versus monster in a battle to the death.

We have little record of what miniature equivalents to these sadistic diversions were engineered to prepare the minds of the youth for a more subtle appreciation of the *vationes*. But we may suppose that smaller mammals and insects provided plenty of scope.

A record does exist, however, of a game played by children in ancient Greece. It is called *The Cockchafer Game*. In this sport, as played by the children of Tarentum, a beetle was tied by a thread, and pulled along the ground in the opposite direction to which it faced. The formula accompanying this amusement was as follows: "I'm leading out my little lame goat." A similar game consisted in tying a piece of cord to the legs of birds, accompanied by this slogan:

Put your foot to the rock,
And out the birds flock.

This game was common in mediæval Britain.

Among peasant folk, the farm-yard hen is, perhaps, the commonest of domestic birds. It is for this reason that the hen and the cock share with the goose and the duck a proverbial imagery of the Irish rural games. Typical of children's interest to a greater measure with poultry than with other animals is a game called *Coilicín coc*:

A group of children stand in a line with their hands upon each other's shoulders. They all face the same way. A robust child is called the Old Hen (*an sean cearc*). Another one, not in the chain, is called *an Coilicín Coc*, the Cock.

The cock and hen then give each other a name, kept a secret between them, e.g. the Hen becomes Maurice, the Cock—Elizabeth.

Now the game starts. The coilicín would come to the Old Hen with a sop, e.g. a pipe, as though he were occupied in smoking it, he would offer a *gal* (pull) to the Old Hen, and so on, right down the line of chickens. The pipe would soon disappear and when the coilicín failed to find it, the fun would begin. He would try to grab the last of the chickens. Meanwhile, the hen:

'Ní bfuigbirse cearc a coilicín cearc
is aoirde mise na coilicín coc
liomsa an lín a coilicín coc.

When he would eventually get one of the line, the prisoner would be asked whom he would prefer, and then the fun would begin! For he would not know who was who: as Maurice would be the Hen, and Elizabeth the Cock! The Cock would then continue until he would grab the last of the chickens. Then both sides would have a test of strength—but the Cock would be victorious at the end.

A relic of tying a bird to a stick or to the hand occurs in an account in a Christmas issue of an ephemeral magazine, *An Cearnog*, of a game in Gaelic which translated means *There Were Two Little Birdeens*. There does not appear, either in Gomme or elsewhere, any foreign precedent for this novel form of play:

bhí dhá éinín ar an bhfal
Ceann aca Seumín, ceann aca Seán,
Eitil leat a Shéimín
Eitil leat a Sheám
Tar ar ais a Shéimín
Tar ar ais a Sheám.

* * *

(*Two little birdeens sitting on the wall,*
One named Peter, and the other named Paul,
Fly away Peter, fly away Paul,
Come back, Peter, come back, Paul.)

Neither the crow nor the blackbird have quite attained that traditional popularity enjoyed in the Nursery Rhyme world by the redbreast and the wren. Robin Redbreast and Jenny Wren have been linked in the child's mind since earliest rockaby days, and in the eighteenth-century toy-books these are eternally linked through *The Marriage of Robin Redbreast and Jenny Wren.*

Whether he inspires random jingles as a result of his proverbial tameness, or arouses the pity of us all through the child's wintry song beginning "The North wind doth blow, and we shall have snow, and what will the Robin do then, poor thing . . .?", this homestead favourite and window-sill squatter is always with us, vaunting his scarlet stigmata, badge of his legendary succour for the Saviour on the Cross.

Robin Robin redbreast
Sits upon a rail;
He nods w' his heid
And wags wi' his tail,

runs the Scottish rhyme. The wren's reputation is discussed in our zodiacal chapter for St. Stephen's Day.[1]

WALLFLOWERS

Wallflowers, wallflowers,
Growing up so high.
We're all pretty maidens (ladies)
Who do not wish to die
Excepting (Polly Baily),
She is the youngest child.
Fie for shame!
Fie for shame!
Turn your back against the game.

[1] p. 207.

HORSE GAMES

Most beloved of all the farm-yard animals or zoo beasts known through the toy-book or the rhyme-anthologies is the horse. We are made conscious of his presence as Dobbin or Dapple Grey while we are still in the cradle. We listen to the tongue-clicking and the trotting sounds by which Nurse or Mother introduces him, before we learn to recognise or repeat that all-important noun in baby language, "Gee-gee".

Very early, also, in our lives are we entertained with the nursery tune to which the words "Ride a Cock Horse to Banbury Cross, To see a Fine Lady on a White Horse" conjure up a fanciful pageantry. This universal favourite is, probably, accompanied by the cantering rhythm of horsemanship—provided by the grown-up's obliging knee.

And our earliest toys? These will, most likely, include some effigy, in one shape or another, of the Friend to Man. Crudely manufactured, on four wheels of sorts, it does not differ much from the selfsame type of animal fashioned by craftsmen in the time of the Pharaohs. Or, harnessed to a wagon, it is made to pull in the same way that the Greeks made their horse-toys draw a chariot. Cavalry mounts made of lead have much in common with the bronze survivals now on view in our museums.

As soon as we are ready to run around and show some enterprise in our play-forms, we are given to know the proud excitement of jumping astride a stuffed replica as large as a colt, or a rocking-horse (61, 63) (becoming more uncommon)—or hobby-horse, according to our social status and Uncle's income!

The hobby-horse is one of the very oldest of playthings. It is recorded that Aegeilias, King of Sparta, who died in 361 B.C., was once taken unawares by a friend when he was playing hobby-horse with his children. He begged his friend not to mention the incident until he had little ones of his own!

Alcibiades, much to his amusement, also surprised Socrates entertaining children in the same way.

Referring to this episode, Mr. Strickland Gibson,[1] in an article on Children's Toys, goes on to describe an old print of the fifteenth century from Holland or Germany, showing the Christ Child riding cock-horse with Saint Dorothy. "The hobby-horse," he says, "consists of a stick with a horse's head to which reins are attached, or merely of a stick with reins. The infant Christ, who is shown riding cock-horse, a very happy conceit, since the hobby-horse may well have been one of the toys actually known to the Christ-Child." (62)

When no such toy was available, the impulse to be mounted and borne across the ground was probably fulfilled through the game of *Pick-a-back*, which is, in fact, a representational game imitating the tournament.

Contests, or races, held between pairs of lads, the one playing the steed, and the other the rider, go back a long time in the annals of human amusement. What wonder then that the image of the horse should have impressed itself so deeply upon the consciousness of most children?

[1] *Country Life*, November 30th, 1940.

Whether through the rhythmic impressions of Nursery Rhymes, the conventional pictures of charger and palfrey in the popular fairy-tale editions, or through the playing of Horse Games, the concept insinuates itself into random doggerel or improvised street rhymes; such as this piece:

As I went up the garden
I found a rusty farthin'.
I gave it to my mother
To buy me a rusty brother.
My brother was too cross
So I put him on a horse.
The horse was a dandy
I gave him a glass of brandy.
The brandy was too strong
I put it in the pond.
The pond was too deep
So I put it in the cradle
And sang it fast asleep.

DRIVING HORSES (64)

I had a little pony
His name was Dapple Grey.
I lent him to a lady
To drive a mile away.
She whipped him and she lashed him,
And she drove him through the mire.
I would not lend my pony again
For all the Lady's hire.

I had a little hobbyhorse
And it was dapple grey.
Its head was made of pea-straw;
Its tail was made of hay.
I sold it to an old woman
For a copper groat;
And I'll not sing my song again
Without a new coat.

The Dapple Grey theme has dramatic undertones. The child identifies itself personally with the pony and the wrong done to it by the heartless borrower. Besides this emotional appeal, the narrative is more coherent than a nursery song; it is tragic but fused by a sense of triumph in the last line.

Among the three Games of Imitation listed under LUDOS in the *Dictionnaire des Antiquités Grecques et Romaines*,[1] is Χαλαμον Περιβῆναι, or Hobby Horses. (The other two happen to be Soldiers and διχαστᾶι, a game of Judges.)

Imaginative modern drawings of museum exhibits of toy horses are included in *A King Penguin Book of Toys*, illustrated by Gwen White. In this fascinating cavalcade of playthings ranging from relics of 2500 B.C. to A.D. 1947, Miss White presents examples of toys in the cultures of Egypt, Turkey, Greece (Thebes), Rome and Britain down the centuries. She depicts horses carved or hacked in wood, made in paper and metal, baked in clay, designed as chargers, tournament mounts, fitted on rollers, struts and rockers, and summarising the

[1] Edited Sahernberg and Saglio.

TOY HORSES

61 From a nineteenth-century print

62 The Christ Child riding Cock Horse with St. Dorothy From a fifteenth-century print

63 From an eighteenth-century painting-book

64 From a German colour lithograph

PLAYING HORSES

continuity of the horse-idea as a basic play-form in every civilisation.

In the Romance languages we find rhymes celebrating the fine points of "The Little Horse". In French and Italian, such jingles are legion. *Cavaluccio, io, io, io* (Gee-up, gee-up, little horsie), introduces the popular Italian version. The vagaries of a mule are the theme of another. Irish juvenile eulogies make much of the "Little Black Ass", a beast proverbially deprived of tribute or pæan, for, although songs galore there are, which sing the praises of "The Little Red Fox" or "The Little Black Hen", the gander or the bumble-bee—poor hairy Neddie is without honour!

Children of Tuscany sing:

Cincirinella had a mule,
All day he drove it in a carriage
He would put on the harness
Trot, my little horse, Yip!

This little rhyming saga symbolises for the child all the romance and excitement suggested by the image "Little Horse".

It is an image which stimulates his imagination, perhaps more than talks of tigers and lions, because it is part of his experience. Horses, whether harnessed to the milk-cart or a brougham cab, a lorry or a gig, or in saddle and bridle, pass by his window every day. The image is pictorial and forceful: the concept of "White Horse" embodies in the child's experience, docility and patience and obedience to his commands—a tremendous emotional joy, expressing the sense that a beast so massive would oblige so tiny a tot. It suggests adventure, speed, the clacking music of shod hooves on the hard surface: the animal's tail in the wind; the excitement of its whinny. The very whiteness of its coat shares, with a magic carpet, the power to transport its imagination into a realm of towered castles, lovely princesses, brave princes and fearful dragons.

Apart from the normal appeal exercised by the idea of the "Little White Horse", in Ireland we find an interesting historical stimulus. It is the unforgettable steed ridden by William of Orange ("King Billy"), who routed the army of James at the now legendary Battle of the Boyne. Possibly it is a protection of this epic, remotely connected with some political itch, that accounts for the plastercast white chargers eternally curving a forefoot from their melancholy vantage points in Dublin's Georgian fanlights—and the theme of the poet Seumas O'Sullivan's famous reflections in *Mud and Purple*.

With these little white statuettes greeting children's wandering gazes, year in and out, it seems natural that several local rhymes have emerged from such play on their fancy. The nursery-rhyme book includes, for example, a curious rhyme that comes from Drogheda. It seems to have some mysterious origin. The very choice of words and the ideas conveyed by them belong to a definition of "pure poetry". No "explanation" has been found for these lines, unless we are prepared to dissolve their poetic essence by suggesting that here the little white horse is part of a table cruet!

Yop, goes the little White Horse,
He can amble—he can trot,
He can rattle the mustard pot![1]

[1] Cf. Robert Ford, *Children's Rhymes of Scotland* (1904), p. 128.

And now, to bring us back to earth, to the realities of the farm-horse and his rustic rollicking driver, here is a game played by Gaeltacht children, known in Irish as *An Lair Ban*, and in English as:

THE WHITE MARE

A group of children gather together, one has a stick and either a *caoidrean* of turf or a potato, or some other object, which they call "The White Mare" or "An Láir Bán". The child who has

the stick must shut his eyes and keep hammering at the caoidrean (or whatever it is) and tries not to let any of the others near it. But they, in their turn, try to steal it (without getting a bang of the stick) and when anybody succeeds, they all shout in one voice at the child who has his eyes shut and is still striking:

Goidead goidead, an láir bán

The child then opens his eyes and says:

Níor goidead riam láir ab'fearr
Annso sear agaib si
Ag doras tighe an gadaide
Is a giolla big bradaig cuir uait an láir bán.

When he says the last line, he draws a blow of the stick on the person whom he suspects of having stolen the white mare. If he guesses rightly, he is allowed to continue chastising his victim, but if he is wrong, the person who really did steal the white mare exlaims: "Cuir uait an Camán", and thereupon takes the stick from the holder and turns it upon him for making a mistake! (*translated from the Gaelic*).

August

"Autumn slips a finger into August," says H. E. Bates. Indeed, this month carries through the first shrivelling leaf its chilling prophecy (65, 67).

For no reason that we can explain, our games for this month all have to do with a gloomy subject, for they are, mostly, Action Songs associated with DEATH and BURIAL.

COCK ROBIN—AN ACTING GAME

Who killed Cock Robin?
I, said the Sparrow,
With my bow and arrow,
I killed Cock Robin. (68)

Chorus

All the birds of the air
Went a-sighing and a-sobbing
When they heard of the death
Of poor Cock Robin,
When they heard of the death
Of poor Cock Robin. (68)

Before we can understand the nature of the violent contrast by which the Games of Weddings and Funeral are juxtaposed, following upon each other in a dramatic performance, we must try to realise what lies behind the child's conception of death, and how it differs essentially from that of the adult.

65 Seventeenth century

66 From a Dalziel original

67 From a series, 1804

KITE FLYING

68 The Burial of Cock Robin
After a painting by W. Collins

Lowenfeld makes the distinction clear in this brief passage: "Children express something very definite with this sort of play, but it is fantasy and not reality. For example, it is clear that killing has another meaning than real death, since in general children playing 'killing' feel it necessary that people killed should come to life again." The emphasis that Lowenfeld lays on the relationship of these games (in which characters "die" and come to life again), to fantasy rather than to reality, is borne out by the researches of Sylvia Anthony. We should, however, allow for elasticity in Lowenfeld's terms of reference. What we, with adult definitions, designate as Fantasy may, for the child, be tantamount to Reality, the greater Reality of kathartitic experience, as contrasted with the humdrum realism of bread without jam, exercise books, quarrels with his or her playmates, pills and punishments.

Let us first consider Sylvia Anthony's conclusions in her work *The Child's Discovery of Death*.

The author undertook her investigation in 1937, when the psychological "position" was as follows. Piaget and others had made it clear that the mind of the child undergoes a fundamental change between the ages of seven and seven and a half. Until then its thought has been egocentric; the world has appeared only in terms of its wish; people, things outside itself, are grasped at with the hand, with the eye, of satisfaction; it has learnt to speak, but its speech is confined to orders and to a running commentary in the third person on its own actions; its reasoning has been intuitive, with the intuition which accepts from older children the "truths" enshrined in the Singing Games; where facts do not suit its train of thought, it invents them, as we may observe in the instances of the Street Rhymes and Sectarian Verses. It seeks to connect everything with everything else, and to justify everything.

In this world, Piaget demonstrated by his precise annotation of childish speech and behaviour, *there is no room for chance*. Singing "happens", Marriage "happens", Dukes, Persons, Princes, Queens, Devils, Heroes and Villains all "happen", without any preconception of *accident*. The minute that the child encounters chance, say, in the extreme form of death (the finding of a dead bird or animal), it ceases to accept death as a natural "happening" that can be arranged, organised, controlled—like Ring o' Roses, or Marriages, or Dressing-up Games. Death, at this stage, becomes an obstacle that cannot be baulked.

At this point, roughly speaking, Piaget left off,[1] and Sylvia Anthony begins, psychological research. Most of the material has been obtained through her tests among L.C.C. school-children, over a period of years. Before we survey the background to the games dramatising burials and death, here is an extract, quoted at random, from the field-data which she examined, in order further to adjust our ideas on the child's attitude to death.

> In its first guises, death may appear innocuously as a falling asleep, a far journey, a disappearance with the hope of return. One child, seeing its mother stretched dead on the floor, lay down beside her and went to sleep; another believes that the person buried will come back to life like a spring flower; to others it means " 'adn't 'ad no dinner"; "When you're in your coffin and you're layin' in it", or, "I would be very sorry, too, if I were dead". In each case, at this stage, Death is regarded as something that can be experienced in terms of living, a step like being married. Later *may* come the idea of finality, the association of Death with old age and with violence. But old age is still a condition of *other people*.

This, then, is the stage at which the playing of Games of Funeral are indulged in by children—the stage before they begin to regard Death as being wrought as a result of chance or violence or powers of Good or Evil.

* * * * *

Of the several Burial Games collected by Gomme, it is of interest that scarcely more than five of these are still played today. They are: *Jenny Jones*, *Poor Mary is a-Weeping*, *Green Gravel*, *Old Roger is Dead* and *Wallflowers*. Many are obsolete like *Booman* and *Little Sally Water*. In Ireland, all five are played. *Old Roger*, although the version which follows was collected in County Down, is fast dying out. *Green Gravel*, once very common in Dublin, is found there no longer. *Wallflowers* alone, with

[1] *The Language and Thought of the Child* and *The Child's Conception of the World*.

To the child at play, Death is less permanent than a soap-bubble (69).

that inexplicable feature that marks out one game for survival as against its fellows, appears to be universally known and thus is handed down from one generation of youngsters to the next.

These are all played as Ring Games, accompanied by melodic chorus:

JENNY JONES

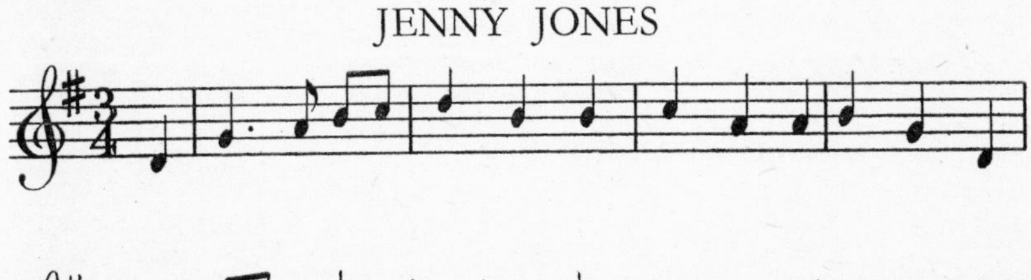

Of this game Bett remarks:

> The name of *Jenny Jones* . . . has suffered many corruptions; in one Scottish version it has become *Genesis* (*We've come to see Genesis, Genesis, Genesis* . . .): a tribute doubtless to the Biblical knowledge of the Scottish child. It ought to be *Jenny Jo*—the old (Scottish) name for a sweetheart, as in "John Anderson, my jo John". . . .

The acceptance of this correction gives us reason to believe that the game also came to Ireland by way of the Scottish settlers in County Antrim.

Here is the conventional version of *Jenny Jones*:

I've come to see poor Jenny Jones,
Jenny Jones, Jenny Jones,
I've come to see poor Jenny Jones,
And how is she today?

She's washing, she's washing, etc.
And you can't see her today.

Very well, ladies, ladies, ladies,
Very well, ladies, and gentlemen too.

I've come to see poor Jenny Jones,
Jenny Jones, Jenny Jones,
I've come to see poor Jenny Jones,
And how is she today?

A change comes into the spirit of the game and the next replies are that she is dying, and then that she is dead. Then the visitors say (receiving answers):

I come in my white dress, white dress, white dress,
And how will that do?

White is for a wedding, a wedding, a wedding,
White is for a wedding and that won't do.

I come in my red dress, red dress, red dress,
I come in my red dress,
And how will that do?

Red *is for soldiers, for soldiers, for soldiers,*
Red *is for soldiers, and that won't do.*

I come in my blue dress, blue dress, blue dress,
I come in my blue dress, and how will that do?

Blue is for sailors, for sailors, for sailors,
Blue is for sailors, and that won't do.

I come in my black dress, black dress, black dress,
I come in my black dress, and how will that do?

Black is for a funeral,
And that WILL do
To carry poor Jenny to the grave.

An interesting reading is the County Down current alternative for verse 8, i.e. "Red's for the English and that won't do".

Gomme (p. 492, vol. XII of 7th Series of Patterson's *Notes and Queries*) quotes seventeen variants of *Janet Jo'*, three being from Ireland, cf. the variants from Belfast, Lismore and County Down. The refrain of the latter, answering the question "What shall we dress her in, dress her in, dress her in?" has an interesting localism. "Shall it be orange" receives from the answering group the reply:

Orange for the Orange-men, the Orange-men, the Orange-men,
And that will not *do.*

In the current Dublin variant they used to substitute the final colours, as follows:

Black is for the Devil, the Devil, the Devil,
Black is for the Devil, and that won't do.

White is for the Angels, the Angels, the Angels,
White is for the Angels, and that WILL do.

The choice of white should have been equally acceptable to the Dublin children! White was the mourning colour in ancient Rome. It is still the conventional colour worn by coachmen on funeral cortèges, and upon the horses' trappings and coachmen's hats, in country parts of Ireland; likewise, in Catholic countries of Central Europe; and also in Russia. It is the ill-omened colour of the dress demanded to be worn by the disobedient children in a French Ring Song, from the Champagne district, entitled *Le Pont de Londres*, as follows:

Sur le pont de Londr' un bal y est donné
Aline demande à sa mère y aller
—Oh! Non, ma fille, aû bal vous n'irez pas:
J'ai fait un songe que vous serez noyée,
Son frère arrive dans un bateau doré.
—Ma sœur, ma sœur, qu'avez-vous à pleurer?
Ma mère ne veut pas que j'aille à bal danser.
—Mets ta robe blanche et ta ceinture dorée.—
Les cloches de Londr' se mirent toutes à sonner,
Sa mère demande pourquoi les cloches sonnaient.
—Votre fille Aline est morte et enterrée,
Voilà le sort des enfants obstinés!

POOR MARY IS A-WEEPING

A Funeral Game, sung to a sweet and haunting melody, is this one. Gomme gives about twenty variants of the song, but none from Ireland: that it was most popular there, and above all in the Dublin back streets (where it still is played), can be deduced from a childhood reference to it by Sean O'Casey in his chapter on Street Games in *I Knock at the Door*:

> Tired of skipping, someone would suggest a ring; and boys and girls, their shyness gone, would join hands in a great ring, a girl, pretending to be weeping with her hands over her eyes, standing in the centre. Older people, the men smoking, the women knitting or gossiping, would stand at the doors, and watch the circling ring, singing as it circled
>
> *Poor Jennie is aweeping, aweeping, aweeping,*
> *Poor Jennie's aweeping, on a bright summer day.*
> *Pray tell us what you're weeping for, weeping for, weeping for,*
> *Pray tell us what you're weeping for, on a bright summer day.*
> *I'm weeping for my lover, my lover, my lover,*
> *I'm weeping for my lover, on a bright summer's day.*

The versions recorded by Gomme come from Surrey, Worcester, Dorset, Norfolk, Berkshire, Lincoln, Staffordshire, Gloucester, Hampshire, Cambridgeshire, South Devon, which would appear to label it as a specific English adaptation. To a detailed analysis chart she adds the following comments on the game:

> . . . the versions are evidently fragments only, and probably one time ended with marriage . . . the incident of weeping for a sailor-lover who was dead (seacoast variants), tells all the more strongly in favour of the original version having represented MARRIAGE and LOVE and not DEATH, but it does not follow that the Marriage Formula belongs to the oldest or most original part of the game. I am inclined to think that this has been added, since marriage was thought to be the natural and proper result of choosing a sweetheart.

Hugh Quinn's manuscripts give the girl's name in the title-line of the Belfast version as Mary.

GREEN GRAVEL

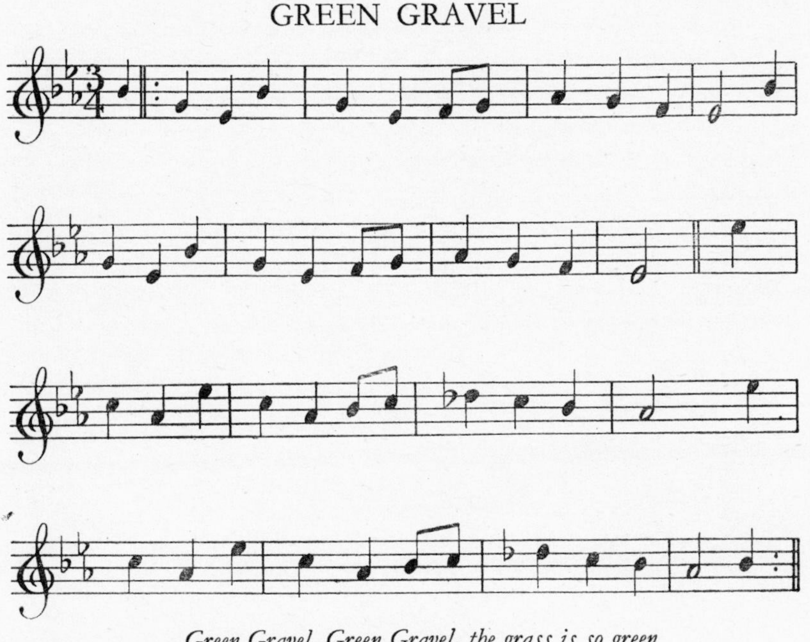

Green Gravel, Green Gravel, the grass is so green
The fairest young damsel that ever was seen.
I'll wash you in milk
And I'll clothe you in silk,
And I'll write down your name
With a gold pen and ink,
O Sally, O Sally, your true love is dead,
He sent you a letter to turn round your head.[1]

This is the orthodox English version of the Singing Game. Gomme cites a Belfast variant submitted by W. H. Patterson which is not more than a local modification of this text. In County Down today, it is still played, though in a varying form, for instance, as follows:

Green Gravel, Green Gravel, your grass is so green,
You're the fairest young damsel that ever I've seen.
I washed her, I dressed her,
I robed her in silk,
And I wrote down her name with a glass pen and ink.

Dear Eileen, dear Eileen, your true love is dead
And I send you a letter to turn round your head.

[1] The score, together with two separate versions of the text, is published in Series III of Novello's *Children's Singing Games*, edited by Cecil Sharp.

An obvious corruption. Yet the English origin of this game is self-evident. Concerning variants Nos. 18, 23 and 25, as examined in her table-analysis, Gomme writes: "The dirge, or singing to the dead, is indicated here, and the beauty of the first line is in complete accord with the mournful music."

Kathleen Freeman, in an essay,[1] describes a Funeral Ring Game played by the children of ancient Greece, entitled *Turtle*. A chorus of girls would circumambulate, one single girl standing in the centre of the human circle, in movement to the following dialogue:

ALL: *Turtle, Turtle, what do you do?*
SHE: *I'm weaving a web of finest hue.*

It developed into:

ALL: *And how came your little one, dead to be?*
SHE: *He drove his white horse into the sea.*

OLD ROGER IS DEAD

The following is a version which I saw played in County Down to a melody and with actions, with the E-I-O sung out most lugubriously as a wail:

Old Roger is dead and he lies in his grave,
Lies in his grave, lies in his grave,
Old Roger is dead and he lies in his grave,
E, I, O.

They planted an apple-tree over his head,
Over his head, over his head,
They planted an apple-tree over his head,
E, I, O.

The apples got ripe and they all tumbled down,
All tumbled down, all tumbled down,
The apples got ripe and they all tumbled down,
E, I, O.

[1] *Greece and Rome*, vol. IV, No. 16.

69 Country Children Playing at Bubbles

70 "Please remember the Grotto"

71 Eighteenth century: after a painting by Goya

72 Twentieth century (during the Battle of Britain)
London Children at a school in Soho

(*Photo Z. Glass*)

THE RING GAME

There came an old woman a-picking them up,
A-picking them up, a-picking them up,
There came an old woman a-picking them up,
E, I, O.

Old Roger got up and he gae her a thump,
Gae her a thump, gae her a thump,
Old Roger got up and he gae her a thump,
E, I, O.

Which made the old woman go hippety-hop,
Hippety-hop, hippety-hop,
Which made the old woman go hippety-hop,
E, I, O.[1]

The respective roles of Old Roger, Apple-Tree and Old Woman, are all interpreted again until the last active episode, when a new cast of players begins the dream all over again. Here again we have the Apple-Tree concept—possibly another importation into Ulster from Gloucestershire. The Fertility symbolism of the playlet is evident too.

Within the Funeral category, Henderson[2] mentions another curious funeral ceremony surviving in a child's game, called *Dish-a-loof*. It is included in this investigation because it seems to be the English equivalent of another game with hands, not mentioned in Gomme's *Traditional Games*. This is the fast-fading game of *Bush-an-auleen*. It is mentioned in an issue of *Irisleabhar na Gaedhilige* for 1889 by a correspondent who noted that it had been a favourite game in County Meath up to thirty years ago, that was, up to 1859:

> Bush an auleen (i.e. *bois anall-in*, the little game of palm hither, hand hither). *A*, usually a small child, held out its hand, palm downwards. Over the back of *A*'s hand, *B* drew lightly his own palm, towards himself, three times, saying:
>
> *Poor Bushanauleen,*
> *Poor Bushanauleen*
> *Big Bushanauleen!*
>
> At the word 'Big' the child, in the course of a short time, learned to snatch away his hand to escape the little slap which *B* dealt *A*'s hand at the third *bushanauleen*. . . .

[1] Kilkeel, February 1942.
[2] *Folklore of the Northern Counties.*

Another relic of the custom of clapping hands at ancient burial ceremonies is the game of *Hiss and Clapp*, now obsolete. It was reported, nevertheless, from County Cork by Mrs. Keane, and hence found a record in Gomme's compendium.

Apart from their ritualistic antiquity, these games of playing with their hands and feet are beloved of children. As much as they are attracted, at a certain age, by playing with mud and water, or by an interest in excreta, so, too, do they manifest an interest in their own limbs, particularly their toes and fingers. Thus the popular trick of interlocking the fingers and making imitation shapes while playing this:

FINGER GAMES

There's the church and there's the steeple!
And here are the doors; and here, the people.
There's the parson walking upstairs!
And here's—the parson saying his prayers!

Or, again, in the world-wide game of *Cat's Cradle*, on which Professor Hadon has made an exhaustive investigation in many countries. He was, nevertheless, unaware that there exists a Gaelic variant of the game, played in the Gaeltacht and known as *An Crinin Cait*. Every baby is taught the Nursery Game played with the toes, i.e. *This Little Piggie went to Market*, etc. Finally, there is the finger-guessing game of *Hunt the Buck* (dealt with on p. 189), and a finger-naming game, as reported in a fore-mentioned Gaelic magazine, and in which the thumb and digits are assigned the following poetical and fanciful names:

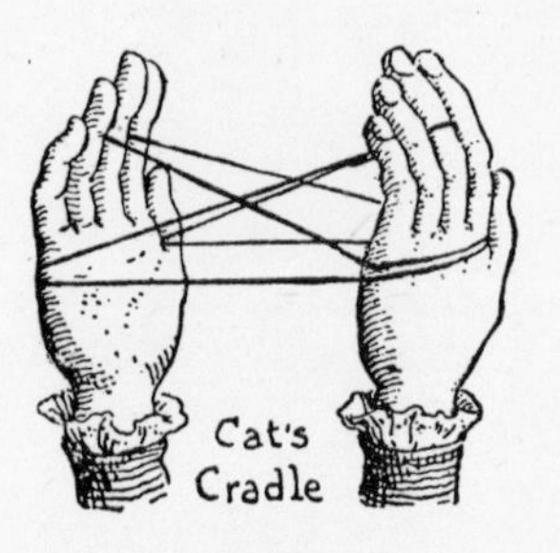

Thumb, Wizbee, Long Man,
Cherry-tree: and Little Jack a'Dandee.

The naming of each toe and finger by children with a separate name goes back to times when each of these was particularly designated. Halliwell gives them in this order:

Thumb
Toucher
Longman
Leche-man
Little-man

and here are some variants:[1]

Essex	*Scotland*	*Lancashire and Cheshire*	
Tom Thumbkin	Thumbkin	Tommy Thumbkin	Bill Milker
Bess Bumpkin	Lickpot	Billy Wilkins	Tom Thumper
Long Linkin	Langman	Long Duster	Long Lazy
Bill Wilkin	Berrybarn	Jacky Molebar	Cherry Bumper
Little Dick	Pirlie Winkie	Little Perky	Tippety, Tippety-Townend

Toes

Toe Tipe
Penny Wipe
Tommy Tistle
Billy Whistle
Tripping-go

TWO FACE RHYMES

Bo Peeper
Nose Dreeper
Chin Chopper
White Lopper
Red Rag
And Little Gap.

* * *

Here sits the Lord Mayor,
Here sits his two men (eyes),
Here sits the cocadoodle (right cheek);
Here sits the hen (left cheek);
Here sits the little chickens (tip of nose);
Here they run in (mouth):
Chinchopper, chinchopper,
Chinchopper, chin! (chuck the chin)

[1] Courtenay Dunn, *Natural History of the Child: Fingers.*

AND A FINGER GAME

This old man, he played one
He played knick-knack on my thumb
Knick knack, Paddy Whack, give a dog a bone
This old man came rolling home.

End of Summer

EPILOGUE ON THE RING GAMES

"*As a rough summary of the Welsh evidence, it may be stated that well-worship in the district occupied by the later of the two Celtic invaders of Britain, is far ruder and more primitive than in districts occupied by the Teutonic invaders of Britain. Either, then, modern culture has acted more powerfully upon Teutonic England than upon Wales, rooting up the pagan rites that existed there, or else Teutonic culture itself acted against the cult of well-worship, and so helped to whittle it down to its* present significance. . . ."

"In Ireland, *well-worship is nearly universal, and the offering of piece of rag is the invariable accompaniment. Among examples of rag-wells, which show the common basis that the cult has in all parts of the British Isles, may be mentioned Ardclinis, Co. Antrim; Errigal-Kerogue, Co. Tyrone; Dungiven; Saint Bartholomew's Well at Filtown, Co. Waterford; Saint Brigid's Well at Cliffony, Co. Sligo; and Rathlogan, in Kilkenny.*"

Ethnology in Folklore, 1892, by George Lawrence Gomme.

"*The locality of wells in Ireland forms a very interesting part of their history. Along the old ways, not infrequently hidden in the fields, we discover interesting localities, with traces of ancient boundaries and primitive plantations, their verdant swards and leafy sweetness at once indicating their venerable old age; and where the progress of modern reclamation has not obliterated the landmarks of previous generations—the peculiar configuration of those places at once points them out as scenes of former life and importance.*"

From the *Processions of the Royal Historical and Archæological Association of Ireland*, 4th Series, 266, 1890.

The Ring Game, *ronde* as it is called in France, and *round* in the Middle English period, is a survival among children of very ancient tribal custom and fertility rituals (72). It is one of the few patterns (i.e. the pattern of the circle, *an fainne*) which have been stamped on Celtic racial memory, as though concentrically, by successive eddies of civilisation. Thus in areas comparatively more free from Anglo-Saxon or Anglo-Norman influence the Ring Game survives in a form essentially Celtic—a form that is ingrained in the native element from pre-Christian times (71).

P. Saintyves,[1] in his thesis on this one aspect of traditional play, maintains emphatically the case for the pagan origin of the Ring Game:

> La plupart des vieilles rondes populaires ont une origine rituelle: leurs chants sont *les incantations* au pouvoir magique, la danse en ronde est une cérémonie de circumambulation, un encerclement, ainsi que le dit si bien le mot anglais qui designe la ronde: *circling*, mais un circlement mystique. Les rondes sont éminemment des créations du viel esprit magico-religieux. . . .

For the purpose of this thesis, all of the premises, and most of the conclusions of the "Magico-religious" school of thought, are unequivocally accepted. No other point of view has such a wealth of conclusive evidence to support it: no other quasi-scientific explanation, whether by the whimsical "spontaneous purists" or by the advocates of geometrical notions in Froebelian educational technique, contain any measure of factuality. The purists, if a few sentimental untrained collectors can merit a scholastic

[1] *Liturgies Populaires*, p. 10.

title, are content to dismiss all antiquarian postulates, in terms somewhat less caustic than those employed by Norman Douglas[1] in an epilogue to his anthology as "sheer tommyrot". Saintyves, on the contrary, had the whole gamut of European data at his disposal, equally in the universities of France as in those of Belgium and Germany, and his conclusions deserve to be regarded with the authoritative respect which such a student commands.

From the above-mentioned extract he proceeds to show that the early Church's hostility towards the dance was based not solely (as certain moralists and sermonisers endeavour to assert) upon the grounds that dancing was often an occasion for licence (a bias which still has a forceful following among a section of the Irish clergy to this day), "but because the dance so frequently led people straight back to ancient pagan rites which they preserved from times immemorial".

Pursuing the argument further, Saintyves,[2] in Chapter II, discusses the magical values of encircling:

> *Circumambulation*, du latin *circum ambulare*, marcher autour, s'éxplique suffisamment par son étymologie. On pratique une circumambulation en tournant autour d'une pierre, d'un arbre, d'un animal, ou d'un être humain, ou, lorsequ'on fait le tour d'un autel, d'une maison, d'un temple ou d'une ville. Les rites de circumambulation ont essentiellement pour but de délimiter, de constituer, de définir le champ d'action, des forces magico-religieuses que l'ont met en œuvre par des actes appropriés.

Here we note the supposed constraining motive in the act of encircling. From this point he goes on to explain the function of singing in the Ring Games:

> Parmi ces actes, les prières et les chants, que l'on appelait jadis des enchantements et des incantations, fournissent un appoint souvent essentiel. L'encerclement ou l'envelopment, car il n'est pas toujours nécessaire de former un cercle géometrique, peut s'obtenir de bien des façons, soit en effectuant un simple tracé superficiel, soit au moyen d'un lien matériel, d'une sorte de chaine ou de ceinture; soit, enfin, au moyen d'un cercle vivant, d'un anneau humain dont tous les

[1] *London Street Games.* [2] Op. cit., p. 23.

individus se tiennent par la main afin de former une véritable chaîne. C'est précisement le cas des rondes populaires.

And an extremely valid case it is, too, especially the conception of *un cercle vivant* (a living circle), and *l'anneau humain* (the human ring).

Bett, in his essay on this subject, draws mainly upon established lines of research, more notably by those writers who insist on the Graeco-Roman origins of the Ring Game. Gomme,[1] on the other hand, whose examination of the Ring Game and its sub-orders is the most thorough ever carried out in the British Isles, suggests a primitive tribal background as the basis of the games:

> The circle games, I consider to be survivals of dramatic representation of customs performed by people of one village or of one town or tribe—representations of social customs of one place or people, as distinct from the 'line' form of games, which represent a custom obtaining between two rival villages or tribes.
>
> Thus, I am inclined to consider the joining of hands in a circle as a sign of amity, alliance and kinship. In the case of the 'line games' hands are clasped by all players on each side. When hands are joined all round, so that a circle is formed, all are concerned in the performance of the same ceremony.
>
> There is no division into parties, nor is difference of opinion shown, either by action or words, in circle games.

The above two extracts, then, briefly illustrate two viewpoints, by no means incompatible, as advanced by two leading students of the subject. But other students have bestowed on scholarship a favour equally as great as have these specialists in doing the work of collecting, annotating, editing and compiling the texts and musical score of these *rondes*. Among them, primarily, Lambert.

Louis Lambert[2] confined his compilation to the *rondes* of Provence and other *régionaliste* examples from France.

Prefacing his collection, complete with musical score of all rhymes sung to tunes, he has contrasted the indigenous Provençal nursery songs with those of the rest of France. He remarks: "Il n'en est de même dans celles des rondes enfantins qui a beaucoup

[1] Vol. II, pp. 478–9. [2] *Chansons Populaires*, vol. I, chap. 2.

emprunté aux chants français. Ces rondes ont subi naturellement des influences extérieures; c'est la conséquence d'un système d'éducation uniforme, du contact des enfants aux écoles, où la langue française est uniquement employée."

IN IRELAND

The same diagnosis may be applied to the Ring Games surviving among Irish children. These, too, have undergone a series of transformations. They have, from the fertility rituals of their pre-Christian forms, sometimes re-emerged as the pastimes of farming communities at harvest-time; as amusements played around a fireside on St. Stephen's Night, or on Hallowe'en; at weddings, wakes and May festivals; in a word, as true folk customs, irrespective of their juvenile prerogative.

Others have much in common with festivals of spring, in which the act of sowing seed is the chief feature. Still others have been transmogrified by a long era of invading strains: Celt, Saxon, Dane, Norman and Lowland Scots, each of which has shaped the contents of the Ring Games between the anvil of traditionalism and the changing hammers of conflicting cultures. This continuous beating and flattening of the shapes has had the effect of revealing, in towns and cities at any rate, that the marks of the latest invader are most visible, and although a Ring Game may have originated in the lands of the Mediterranean, and, indeed, even earlier, in the lands of the Nile, and introduced to these islands either by the Roman soldiers or the early Celts who preceded them, it is the Anglo-Saxon feature, complexion and metric of the games which are uppermost.

In the seventeenth, eighteenth and earlier nineteenth centuries the Planter influence predominates. From Planter stock first emanated the robust Elizabethan English which still persists in Irish communities whilst it has become moribund in many English centres, London particularly. From Planter stock came the English *round*, and the simple dances which, later, were frowned upon by the Puritans (103). Likewise, from Planter stock was imported the idea of holding hands in a ring, a custom followed in most lands on the continent of Europe.

As a substratum to these influences one must stress the native Gaelic tradition of the *fairy ring*, and the dance associated with it. Folklorists working in the Gaeltacht areas have established points of resemblance and coincidence between the Irish Fairy Dances and those surviving among other Celtic peoples. While Kennedy,[1] in a different context, offers a vivid comparison with the Breton *korils-ronde*. He furthermore, despite his day and age, shows no hesitation in taking for granted the pagan sources of these customs. In this connection he instances the charming legend telling how the hunchback supplied the last line to an inconsequential fairy rhyme overheard one day in the form of a haunting melody near a dell frequented by the Good People:

Dia luian, dia Mairt,	*Moon's Day, Mar's Day,*
Dia luian, dia Mairt,	*Moon's Day, Mar's Day,*
Dia luian, dia Mairt,	*Moon's Day, Mar's Day,*
Agus Dia Ceadoin.	*And Woden's Day, too.*

* * * * *

From this survey we may move forward to examine the Ring Games that still survive among Irish children today.

The most commonplace of all Ring Games which have an accompanying rhyme seems to be *Ring o' Ring o' Roses, a pocket full of posies*. It is usually played by very, very young children and is doubtlessly a survival of some old fertility chant. Bett maintains that the final words, "Ash-er, ash-er, ash-er", should read "A-tisha" (three times) and that they indicate an explosion of pretended sneezing. The sneeze, he attempts to show, has a

[1] *Legendary Fictions* (1886), p. 104.

close magical connection with the human spirit. In his discussions he nevertheless omits to cite the Gaelic custom of exclaiming "Dia linn" (God bless you!) when a child sneezes.

Lambert gives six versions of a Provençal *ronde* similarly addressed to "Rousie" (Fr. le rosier, the rose-tree). They are all short rhymes. The line equivalent to our exclamation "Ash-er", etc., "we all fall down", has an interesting parallel movement in Ronde No. III as quoted by Lambert:

(French version)
"*Branle, calendre,*
La Fille d'Alexandre
La pêche bien mûre,
La figue bien mûre,
Le rosier tout fleuri,
Coucou toupi!

En disant '*coucou toupi*', tous les enfants, qui forment la ronde, accroupissent."

This falling-down gesture is common to all versions played in Ireland. In County Donegal the whole point of the amusement has shifted to the recital of the word "pop" in the last line of the variant played there:

Here we go round the Jingo Ring,
Jingo Ring, Jingo Ring,
Here we go round the Jingo Ring
And the last pops *down!*

In a manner as concentrated as the most economically worded eclogue, these Ring Games express the feeling at the back of such play-patterns, namely, the consciousness of nearness to the earth, to the ground where growth is taking place; to elemental seasonal changes on the tree, like flowering, fruiting and ingathering of the crop; and it is, assuredly, this primal awareness of fertility on the earth that makes the whole body of ring games kin.

In Italy the game is invariably played round a tree. The English Ring Game, *Here We Go Round the Prickly Pear*, is an example nearer home, for the purpose of evaluation in the light of Fraser's *Golden Bough*. The Tuscan version of the Italian rhyme offers an intriguing comparison as to the similarity of metre, if in nothing else:

Gira, gira, tondo,	*Round and round the ring,*
Il pane sotto il forno . . .	*The bread is under the oven,*
Un mazzo di viole,	*A bunch of violets,*
Le dono a chi le vuole,	*I'll give them to whoever wants 'em*
Le vuela la Sandrina	*Sandrina wants them*
caschi la più piccina![1] (47)	*let the smallest fall.*

The editor's footnote to this Tuscan rhyme is as follows: "La cantano i bambini tenendosi per mano in modo da formare un circolo: all'ultimo verso la più piccina si china poi si ricomincia da capo." The incongruity of the narrative is typical of all children's rhymes.

In warmer climates, where continuous sunshine adds a vernal quality to the lives of small children, most of these Ring Games are invocations to some form of growth, but in the temperate zone, local conditions do, necessarily, bring about adjustments in the text. The following version comes from a very ancient fishing settlement exposed to the east wind:

Snowy weather, frosty weather,
When the wind blows
We all fall together!

In the Gaelic periodical *Locrann*[2] is found a printed version of *Ring o' Roses* in Irish, but without any description of the movements:

Bulla! Bulla! Baisín,	*Clap! Clap! Hands,*
Ta'n bo sa gùirdín	*The cow is in the garden*
Síos libh!	*Down ye go!*
Síos libh!	*Down ye go!*
Éirigidh anois Eirigidh!	*Get up now, get up!*
Déanam arís é	*Let's do it again.*
Bulla! Bulla! Baisín.	

Another Ring Game, surviving generally in Ireland, is the following:

Three times around goes the galley, galley ship,
Three times around goes she,
Three times around goes the galley, galley ship,
And she sinks to the bottom of the sea (sitting action).
Pull her up! Pull her up! says the galley, galley ship,
And she sinks to the bottom of the sea.

[1] Oddone, *Cantilene Populari dei Bimbi d'Italia.*
[2] *Nodlaig,* (1926) (Christmas Number), p. 99, col. 2.

A variant of this from County Tyrone is as follows: "Girls stand in a long line holding hands. Last player touches the wall. First player walks around and dips under the arch formed by the last player's hand, followed by the rest of the line. They continue like this until the last player's arch is completed. Then they all unravel to this tune:

The big ship sails through the alley, alley, O,
The alley, alley, O, the alley, alley, O,
The big ship sails through the alley, alley, O,
On the fourteenth of December."

Another Ring Game, with a suspicion of the Courtship motif about it, is *In and Out the Window*. A game most widespread in Dublin. In his chapter "The Street Sings", O'Casey gives an account of its rules: ". . . the ring would stand still with arms held high while a player would dart in and out of the ring under the upraised arms as the circle of boys and girls sang in a livelier metre:

In and out the window, in and out the window, in and out the window,
As you have done before,
Stand and face your lover, stand and face your lover, stand and face your lover,
As you have done before.

Shy, grey-eyed Jennie Clitheroe, with her curly head hanging, stood before Johnny . . . his face went scarlet as he heard the titters of the ring:

Chase him all round Dublin, chase him all round Dublin, chase him all round Dublin,
As you have done before . . ."[1]

One viewpoint is that "windows" is a corruption of "willows" a tree growing near water and therefore likely to be sacred. In the Belfast version we have "In and out the valley", and in the

[1] *I Knock at the Door*, p. 20.

variant collected by Hugh Quinn it used to be "Go round and round the valley", with the successive lines being "O stand and face your lover", etc., and "Chase him/her back to Scotland", as a prelude to a pursuit by the party appointed in the course of the game! This allusion to "back to Scotland" could have an interesting etymological bearing on our subject.

In a Dublin variant, still very popular among girls at school, the game takes a different form, i.e. tapping on the shoulder, but preserves its basic reference to a type of flower, this identification between maiden and flower being of particular interest in the case of *Wallflowers*, which is examined in the July chapter.

(*a*) *In and out those saucy bluebells*
In and out those saucy bluebells
In and out those saucy bluebells
I am the Master.
Hipper-apper-apper on my shoulder
Hipper-apper-apper on my shoulder
Hipper-apper-apper on my shoulder
I am the Master.

(*b*) *In and out those fairy bluebells*
In and out those fairy bluebells
In and out those fairy bluebells
Aon, do, tri.
Tap a little girl upon the shoulder
Tap a little girl upon the shoulder
Tap a little girl upon the shoulder
Aon, do, tri.

This Ring Game has a particularly sweet melody accompanying it. The linking of arms occurs again in another example widespread in rural places—the game *High Windows*, or *High Gates*: (*a*) Kennedy mentions it as *High Gates*; (*b*) Gomme, on the other hand, quoting her County Leitrim observer, gives it as *High Windows*, "a variant of Drop Handkerchief and Black Doggie". Here are the two references respectively:

(*a*) We cannot afford space for a full description of *High Gates* or *Thread the Needle*, but these healthy and livelier sports are more generally known, all catching hands in a circle and one chasing another in and out under the linked arms of the players. The smaller boys would be occasionally admitted into these reunions.[1]

(*Hedge School.*)

(*b*) Boys hold hands and go round in ring form. One player stands in the middle and strikes one of those in the ring with a bit of grass; both players then run out of the ring and the boy who was in the midst must go round three times. At the third time the boys all cry out "High Windows!", raising their hands at the same time to let the two inside the circle.[2]

[1] *Dublin Univ. Mag.* (1862), p. 608.

[2] Gomme, *Games*, vol. II, p. 429.

A Ring Game based upon the poem by William Allingham, *The Fairies*, with its first line "Up the airy mountain", occurs in Patterson's *Antrim & Down Glossary*. It is probably a corruption of some existing form, fused with the school-book stanzas by Allingham, a popular poet whose lyrics are perhaps the most easily comprehensible in these poetry texts. It is still played in County Down, and here is a contemporary version of it:

Up the heathery mountain
And down the rushy glen
We dare not go a-hunting
For fear of little men.
Up the river and down the lea
That's the way for Billy and me.

Another improvised song, popular in parts of Dublin, is the following:

When I was young and had no sense
I thought I would come to tea,
And when the kettle was boiling
I sang a Chinese song,
Skinny-I-am, goody-I-am,
Come to Chinese supper,
Stick your nose in butter,
Sugar and tea!

This is characteristic of Dublin children's directness and impertinence. The first line is borrowed from the English nursery rhyme that continues with "I bought a fiddle for eighteenpence"; but the second line is probably an echo of a rapscallion street-song, in vogue in South Dublin about 1920–5,[1] incorporating the most atrocious doggerel and opening with:

When I was young and in my pride
I thought I would go to sea,
I sailed upon a pirate ship
That was bound for the Arigho[2] *Sea . . .*

A Ring Song with another original jingle, one recorded by Hugh Quinn[3] as having been current in the streets of Belfast about thirty years ago, is *Hal-a-go-lee*. It is obviously a variant of the English Ring Game *Hobie Hight*:

[1] Daiken, "Only Juvenilia", *Dublin Magazine* (1939).
[2] Arigho was a well-known local Italian family name.
[3] MS. collection.

Hal-a-go-lee, go-lee,
Hal-a-go-lee, go-lo,
Hal-a-go-lee, go-lee,
All on a summer night, O.
Put your left foot in,
Put your left foot out,
Shake it, and shake it, and shake it,
Then turn right round about.

It may also be a corruption of *Lubin*, a Ring Game which Gomme[1] shows as being native to Norfolk, Dorset, Doncaster, London, Oxford and Derbyshire. The Belfast version which she gives in her analysis is:

Here we come looby, looby,
Here we come looby light,
Here we come luby, luby,
All on a Saturday night.

A Ring Game of more agrarian interest, one unrecorded by any of the collectors, occurs today in places as far from each other as County Antrim and County Tipperary:

Mother, will you buy me a milking can,
A milking can, a milking can?
Mother, will you buy me a milking can?
With my one, two and three.

The game proceeds in the form of a dialogue between the chorus and the girl in the centre of the ring, with the last line recurring as a refrain:

Where will the money come from?
Come from, come from,
Where will the money come from?
With my one, two and three.

Sell our father's feather bed,
Feather bed, feather bed,
Sell our father's feather bed,
With my one, two and three.

Where shall the father lie,
Father lie, father lie,
Where shall the father lie,
With my one, two and three.

In the girls' bed,
The girls' bed, the girls' bed,
In the girls' bed,
With my one, two and three.

[1] *Games*, vol. I.

Where shall the girls lie?
Girls lie, girls lie,
Where shall the girls lie?
With my one, two and three.

In the boys' bed,
The boys' bed, the boys' bed,
In the boys' bed,
With my one, two and three.

Where shall the boys lie?
Boys lie, boys lie,
Where shall the boys lie?
With my one, two and three.

In the washing tub,
Washing tub, washing tub,
In the washing tub,
With my one, two and three.
(End)

A notion presenting as much opportunity for *double-entendre* as for that sense of assertive juvenile rivalry between the sexes which receives so much satisfaction from the intoned rhyme:

What are little boys made of?
What are little boys made of?
R*ats and snails and puppy dogs' tails,*
That's *what little* boys *are made of!*

September

The approach of autumn, with its fruity and nutty atmosphere, invests the woods with a special magic. This is also the time of the harvest of natural playthings: fruit-stones, cherry-pips, crabs (76), oak-apples, beech-mast; hazel-nuts, cones, burrs and berries; shells and pebbles, dried peas and beans . . . the pockets become crammed with all things dinkie and diminutive, for bowling and rolling, for flipping and flicking, for tipping and throwing—Nature's tokens. There is a dominant sadness in the season's mood also, colouring the scores of lovely rhymes and games connected with NUTS, RIPE FRUITS and BERRIES (75, 77, 78).

IN THE WOODS

THE GIPSIES

My mother said that I never should
Play with the gipsies in the wood,
The wood was dark; the grass was green;
In came Sally with a tambourine.

I went to the sea—no ship to get across;
I paid ten shillings for a blind white horse;
I up on his back and was off in a crack,
Sally, tell my mother I shall never come back.
(Quoted by Walter de la Mare from Mrs. Lyon.)

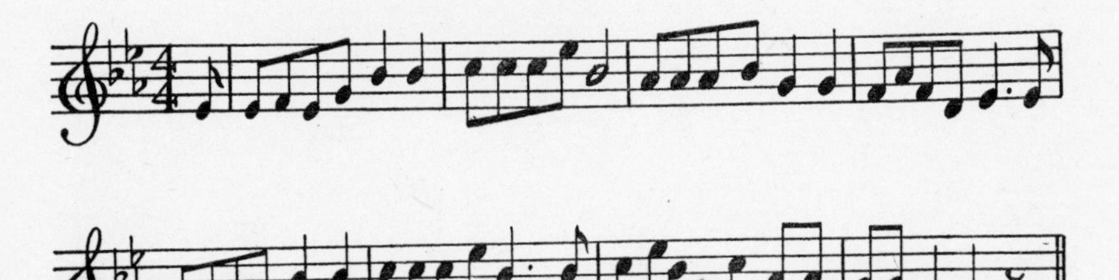

AN OLD NURSERY SONG

I had a little Nut Tree
Nothing would it bear
But a silver nutmeg
And a golden pear.

The King of Spain's daughter
Came to visit me,
And all because of
My little Nut Tree.

I skipped over the water,
I danced over the sea,
And all the birds in the air
Could not catch me.

The poignant story suggested by the cryptic words of this old song, has intrigued, and still fascinates, critics. I have heard many pet theories expounded, purporting to show a link between

the words and the episode of history to which they are thought to allude. Investigations led me to a house outside Cork City, Ronayne's Court, where popular legends say, a giant walnut tree once grew. On the stone fireplace is a Coat of Arms carved by the founder, Morris Ronayne, in 1672. It depicts a tree with six branches, rather like a walnut, set in a barrel, with a little bird on the top, and two nude figures beside the bole. This drawing is a copy of one which the present owner, Mrs. Marie Lucy, sent me. The theory is exciting, but I am not satisfied that there is a definite connection, nor would I be, until three further lines of research are followed and converge. (One would be to establish a link between the House of Ronayne and King Charles I.) Moreover, Miss Mary Ryan, who is well informed on local folklore, has failed to find any conclusive evidence.

A FERTILITY SONG

A rosy apple, a lemon and a pear,
Bunch of roses she shall wear
Gold and silver by her side,
I know who will be the bride.

Take her by the lily-white hand,
Lead her to the altar,
Give her kisses—one, two, three—
Mrs. (child's name) daughter.

Waving good-bye to the swallows and warblers, all set for their long trip to Africa, enters September! September, bringing the milky ears, the golden stooks, the fieldmice. This month means fun and games in the harvest fields, traditional dancing in the countryside, jokes and jollities connected with the Harvest Home (100).

This is also the time of the harvest of natural playthings (73). Mellow fruitfulness has filled the child's junk-crammed pocket with oddments (79) that become more precious than jackdaw's hoard or squirrel's granary. These are Nature's tokens, her discs, coils and counters, her buttons, beans and marbles, which she bestows every autumn, lavishly and with unfailing regularity, upon all those whose little hands cannot forgo a desire to clasp and fondle them.

There, under the oak-trees, are acorns; fascinating valuables, knick-knacks beautifully shaped like cup and egg, refusing to be ignored. Who can resist wanting to pick them up from the ground, turn them in the hand, caress them with the fingers—or slip one into the pocket with a feeling that sometime, somewhere, it will realise its vague but incalcuable value?

Aided by a strong wind, or by a stick thrown among the branches, will fall the swollen spiky shell of the horse-chestnut. With a soft *clump*, as resonant of this season as any plop of trout in water, the shell splits open on the grass to reveal, immaculately cased in its white inner pith, that varnished mahogany-looking nut which soon becomes the prize and preoccupation of every class of lad, and lad of every class—the Conker.

Strung together on a long cord, and caught around the chest like a bandolier of polished brown leather—what a magnificent possession! After the midsummer holidays is the logical time for parading new gadgets on the return to school, the time of new stunts and crazes. The conker fashion catches on and passes from one to another like wildfire. Few games in a playground will hold a group of onlookers in such rapt attention as the contest between nut challenger and nut challenged. Like pendulums they sway at the end of their bits of string, and few can foretell which one will prove to be champion in this struggle for the boast of the survival of the toughest. Generally, but not universally, an accepted jingle is prelude to the smacking, hacking, cracking, whacking game of skill:

Hick, hack, first smack,
Conqueror of eleven!

The game is one of the Conquest group, like *King of the Castle* in origin, combined with a game improvised with the aid of nuts. It has remained very popular. Seasoning the nut, boring a hole through it with nail or spike or gimlet, threading it, preserving it, safeguarding it from the covetous or the tempter—all of this is part of the ritual and its mystery. Sometimes a veteran conqueror will be kept till the following year by some far-sighted strategist. By then it certainly will have become "a hard nut to crack"!

Obli O, my first go!
Obli onker, my first conker!

Prue, in *Precious Bane*, you will remember, tells about a local variant of this open-air game: ". . . Conkers, maybe you know, are snail-shells, and children put the empty ones on strings and play like you play with chestnut cobs. Our woods were a grand place for snails and Gideon has conker matches with lads as far away as five miles the other side of Plash. . . ."

It is now, also (when the picking of a successful fruit crop sets children's thoughts on the fun that will be theirs some two months hence), that at Hallowe'en parties the game of *Bob Apple* is put on the programme.

Games with fruit-stones are legion. They vary with the folklore of a definite locality, and with the children's power of invention. Foretelling the sort of career one will follow, wife or husband wed, house live in, number of children beget, and so on, belongs to the Oracular group in origin; and, although associated equally with Skipping Games or Petal Pulling, with the gibberish of Counting-out Rhymes and what-not, the same old recurring formula of "Tinker, Tailor, Soldier, Sailor" is the very first thing a child blurts out whenever he has occasion to arrange the stones of plum, damson or cherry in a neat row in front of him, or, at the indoor meal, in the shape of a circle or semicircle around the edge of his dessert plate.

And now to stones proper. Most children are fascinated by them. Smooth, rounded pebbles have a deep æsthetic appeal. Even the boy David, as the Bible tells us, carried in his pouch a supply of small stones which one can imagine he was disposed to use for less drastic purposes than the eventual slaying of Goliath. They are the playthings of Tom, Dick and Harriet, available to rich and poor alike. They cost no fancy prices and are not confined to any one area. In some rural areas they take the place of hopping ball in such old favourites as *Ball in the Cap*, or *Ball in the Decker*. Still played in country districts, the game of *Duck at the Table*, according to Patterson,[1] was "a boy's game played

[1] *County Down Glossary.*

73 Nature's Playthings

74 Apple Gathering

76 Crab-apple Harvest

75 Blackberrying

77 Wild Fruits (Sloes)

78 Nutting

with round stones and a table-shaped block of stone". Norman Douglas lists over forty games played with stones which he collected in the London streets prior to 1914. Typical of the data he tabulated in his catalogue is the following extract: ". . . Other stone games are *French Packet* and *Shuffling the Money* and *Five-Ten* and *Hesling* and *Two and Three Holes* and *Knocking Threes* and *Penny Tuppence* and *Stone Chase* and *Throwing Out* and *Ringing the Stone* and *Pudding* and *Ducking Mummy*. . . ." All have, characteristically enough, names incomprehensible except to the initiated.

The chip used in hopscotch, christened a "Piccy" or a "Piggy" or "Pearie", has been mentioned in a previous chapter (p. 42).

Stones, of course, will have become less easy come by, as a result of synthetic and macadamised road surfacing in city districts but they are still the most common form of diversion in the neighbourhood of gravel-pit, quarry, river-bank, or sea-shore (80). Odd little bits of stone with a peculiar feature in shape or colouring excite the child's mind. Be they of veined marble or common grey limestone, perforated sandstone or glossy white silica, they are alike pocketed—to be carried off and to be sold perhaps as sweeties in a game of *Shops*, or used as birds' eggs in a game of *Farm-yards*, whilst fragments of glass and earthenware worn smooth by sea-water are made to represent all manner and means of things connected with playing *House* or *Doll's House*. If they are jagged chips of flint or granite they will soon suggest a host of uses, the flakes of silvery mica being exceedingly attractive, and suggestive of precious metals.

At the water's edge they provide miniature cannon-balls for bombarding paper flotillas, or, more recently, H.E.s in battles fought along the lines of combined operations! Here, too, a suitably shaped piece of stone or slate has only one immediate meaning for a boy—something to send skimming along the surface of lake or harbour, bouncing elastic-like in a fantastic ballet movement that gives endless delight to the aimer.

Played by children on the beach is *Cockshy*, or *The Cockshot Game*, in which an oblong stone is used as a pivot for a series of smaller ones, forming a sort of pyramid. Ammunition stones are hurled at this target from an agreed distance. To aim skilfully,

much after the style of skittles, the question of scoring being arbitrary, seems to be the chief object of this amusement.

In West Cork they have a version of a cricket game called *Tip and Run*; here is a player's account of it:

> A large stone, very flat, is placed standing on its edge, supported behind by a stick, or another stone. A smaller stone is placed flat on the ground several yards away. The ball is bowled along towards the wicket, the batsman hits it and runs to tip. He must touch the flat stone with his bat. Fielding is as in cricket. The player who puts the batsman out, wins.

Incidentally, cricket itself, so incontrovertably accepted everywhere as being a typical Anglo-Saxon sport, has a very near Celtic ancestor. It is a game called simply *Stones*,[1] a description of which may be read by those disposed to argue over the case in an 1830 report from C. H. Kinahan, one of Lady Gomme's voluntary folklore workers, and published in her *Traditional Games* (see p. 24).

The placing of stone upon larger stone has an age-old symbolism. Ritual among primitive peoples abounds with it. The supernatural forces that were inexplicable to ancient man somehow got linked in his mind to the powers of stones. Stones had magical properties. Petros. La pierre druidique. The pagan god-stone. Lapis . . .

[1] See also *Quates*, p. 26.

Before people got theories as to why and how things came to be, ideas built up on the sciences (geology, physics, evolution and so forth), it is easy to imagine what an incomprehensible thing a stone must have been. There it was, a thing complete, unalterable, self-sufficient, something that just . . . that just was! Mythology is full of allusions to it: folklore of all nations is rich with notions contrasting and connecting tree and stone. These are concepts of animate and inanimate, of living growth and dead matter. The one symbolises things temporal; the other is unattached, without roots, without life, change, age. Stone—the only object they knew that could be held within the grasp of actuality, yet in its composition and source as inexplicable and inscrutable as sun, sky, wind or water.

Of all the Stone Games on record, the one which has preserved its essential characteristics over the longest period is perhaps *Fivestones*. In London streets it is called *Knucklebones*; in communities with a peasant background, Scotland and Ireland, they call it *Jackstones*. In Gaelic-speaking outposts—*Sgreaga*.

Artists of the Low Countries (87) have traditionally taken a marked interest in the portrayal of children in naturalistic poses, than which there can be few more engaging than those in the act of dashing about in a market-square or grouped in a huddle about some form of game going on in a country site.

In the Douce Collection at Oxford's Bodleian Library you can see scores of old prints showing Flemish children at play. Some of these are from the collection of pictures by Jacob Cats, published in 1625[1] (88). It shows, all told, thirteen separate games, with marbles being played in the centre foreground. This

[1] *Houwelick: A Book of Emblems.*

print, which varies with different editions of the album and must have been extremely popular, shows Dutch children in the act of bowling hoops, running with paper windmills, flying kites, whipping tops, flying captive birds, inflating a football bladder, arranging a doll's house, blowing bubbles, playing at horses and soldiers, standing on the head, walking on stilts, skipping, riding the hobby-horse, shooting skittles (85), leap-frog and that old favourite—*Blind Man's Buff*: doing, in fact, exactly the same things that, our records show us, were being done by children in Britain at that time and in that century.

In one of the variants, skating and sliding are shown, thus detracting from the seasonal nature of the composition. Also here you will see a 1642 printing of "Hovwelick", being a fine example of the engraver's art (87). In this particular picture, almost every then-popular game is depicted *except* marbles, for some incredible reason!

Yet marbles was a game that caught the imagination of the early Flemish and Dutch schools of painters. Their studies are a link in an unbroken European pastime that survived the upheavals of Greece and Rome, as they survived the total evacuation of London's children during the anti-Nazi war—children who took with them the pre-war treasures (as though they were connected with a sacred rite) to the remote corners of the Midlands, Wales and other evacuee schooling areas.

The love of marbles led to many a thrilling contest being switched from blitzed streets in Dockland to some village green. I remember witnessing an unforgettable international session on the playground roof of an L.C.C. school in Soho, when the buzz-bomb terror was at its height. Playing, up there above the West End's hooting traffic, were children of parents lately come from France, Belgium, Austria, Palestine, Cyprus, West Africa, and Gibralterians in scores—all Spanish-speaking. It was at this time a magazine editor whom I had interested in the subject, commissioned that ace photographer, Zoltan Glass, to take some action pictures of the wartime twentieth-century child at play. They are a testimony to that unpublicised interchange of folk-games and folklore which are the peculiar heritage of the young (86).

Marbles, more likely as not, are a development of a very ancient

79 A Forerunner of the Yo-yo

80 Gathering Sea-shells for Games

81 Playing Buttons
From an eighteenth-century engraving

82 "The Cheat at Marbles"
From a French series *Les Jeux d'Enfants*, 1850

game. Whether their remote ancestors were smooth and rounded like pebbles, or happened to be chestnuts, cobs, or the stones of cherries and peaches, is really not so important. They may have originated even as birds' eggs. An expert on these matters, Strutt, in his book *Sports*, declares that marbles are quite a modern invention and that they derive their name from *marble*, the substance from which bowls were formerly made, and that their natural precursor was, therefore, the game of bowls, such as Drake proverbially played at Plymouth Hoe! Yet before bowls

ever came on the scene, a Roman Emperor played something very akin to marbles with the children of his own palace.

Among street games they ranked as the most popular in Victorian England, and were always the most democratically enjoyed. Norman Douglas, in his *London Street Games* of 1916, lamented the fact that marbles seemed, even in those days, to be on the decline. Several varieties known to him when a lad had long ago been lost to juvenile memory. Yet, in spite of wartime priorities and post-war manufacturing diversions, the supply still persists, and the impulse to play still craves satisfaction. The names of the forms may change. Indeed, they do so. Would our grandfathers ever have dreamed that their "stonies" might have been superseded by those inevitable products of the steel age, "steelies"—which are merely the craft-name adopted for larger ball-bearings? And shall we ourselves not have a right to expect that plastic marbles in various designs and tinted may be put on the market one fine day not so far off?

Epochs of struggle in humanity's lifeline, wars, upheavals, revolutions may effect a temporary black-out on game-patterns, but they never erase them. Is it not typical that this age-old game should have received from the present generation (so well versed in the technicalities of aircraft construction) the title of "bombers"—which is played by dropping a metal marble plomb from the eye and straight on to an agreed ground target?

Country places offer the game a better chance of survival. But mechanisation, the increase of youth clubs, withdrawal to indoor shelter during the black-out, and other vicissitudes that beset a war generation, have by no means throttled it. To this day, you

will come across children of all social classes, from the richest to the poorest, kneeling to flick the rolling marididdles in city play-centres, back alleys and main roads alike. Endless delight is experienced. In the foremost place, this is an "unorganised" game. It is communal, but in spirit, highly individualistic. Spontaneous, exciting, seasonal, it seems to be inherited mysteriously, without apparent instruction or tutelage, like innate knowledge among primitives, or the homing sense among certain birds. It may even miss a six-year generation altogether—and reappear, presto!

In addition to an intrinsic skill, well tried and tested daily, the game has an added attraction. It boasts of its own vocabulary, its craft ethics, and a conservative love of traditional fashions and local tricks. In pursuing this form of amusement a boy may, in addition to the fun of the thing, develop a gambler's instincts, a strong acquisitive sense, or an exploiter's greed. Many a big monopolist or wealthy magnate might today look back to the

83 Musicians at the Cottage Door—Children Playing Marbles, Foreground
From an original by Adriaen Van Ostade (1610-1685)

[*British Museum*

days when as a whippersnapper he devised ways and means of accumulating all the capital from little Johnny Jones, in a series of do-or-die contests, at a game of *Follow*. In the course of this innocent hobby the nicest of children can evolve sharp practices. And those earnest moralists of the last century, ever ready to use an illustration for didactic purposes, didn't miss the opportunity of issuing an engraving as a warning to naughty little boys (82).

Dutch and Flemish painters of the sixteenth and seventeenth centuries took a delight in painting homely themes. Less doctrinaire than our Victorians, they loved the game subject for its own sake; for, what more typical scene of a happy household than a child being intensely absorbed in a game of marbles? The intrinsic lack of self-consciousness in a pose is achieved; the bended knee, the rapt expression. In city streets or farmhouses this atmosphere of informality is cleverly conveyed, as, for instance, the Adriaen Van Ostade painting called "Musicians at a Cottage Door" (83). So much of a cult, almost, did the painting of children at play become among the Dutch and Flemish that we find Pieter Brueghel devoting a huge canvas exclusively to popular traditional games played by contemporary youngsters.[1]

The game came to England, however, not as might be thought from the Netherlands or France, but rather through the channels whereby it was introduced into those countries, e.g. by the Roman legionaries.

The types of globular baked clay or stones that we see today may be a comparatively modern invention, but their true antecedents were certainly the water-worn pebbles that could be easily bowled along the smooth-tiled courts of ancient Rome. We have the authority of Suetonius that the Emperor Augustine used to enjoy playing some such game with the young Roman lads of his own palace.

Other variants were the stones of cherries and the large pips of soft fruits and nuts of all kinds, including the nut most found in Britain—the hedgerow hazel. Ingenuity varied with season and locality, and the substituting of thick buttons (81) in marble games is on record, too. An aiming game, involving similar movements as those employed in marbles is played in parts of

[1] *Kinderspiele*, Vienna Art Museum.

Ireland and is called *Blind Man's Taw*. Patterson, in his *Antrim and Down Glossary*, confirms that it was played with the eggs of small birds. "The boys place the eggs on the ground, and a blindfold player takes a number of steps in the direction of the eggs; he then aims at them three times in the hope of breaking them. Then the next, and so on."

The toy market which has undergone such complete changes within the past twenty years needs to be studied through a special investigation before facts relating to the manufacture, supply, distribution and demand for marbles could be discussed. But they would make a fascinating subject for research. With the advent of the mechanical toy and stream-lined modern vehicles and armour, marbles, together with old-fashioned things like skittles, wooden tops and wooden hoops have suffered from the fashions of the day, and in big cities—wherever else—are taking a back place.

Our grandfathers enjoyed a much more varied assortment of the playthings than do children nowadays. Prized above every other sort, and, indeed, with the pre-eminence justified on account of the exquisitely beautiful veining of some of them, were the marbles made of agate. They had rich and harmonious colouring. Then there was a sort known as "alleys". They were made of white marble, striped and hued with red, and when the latter predominated, they were called "blood alleys". Next in value to blood alleys ranked "taws" (84) or "stonies". They were of brown marble, streaked with darker tones of the same colour. Next came "French taws" of stained or coloured marble; gaudy Dutch marbles of glazed clay, painted either yellow or green and ornamented with stripes of a dark colour. The very lowest class were "commoneys", held in little repute by those who could procure superior kinds, and were made of unpretentious English clay!

In Dickensian England these were practically a household word. The famous Court scene in *Pickwick* where Sergeant Buzfuz, speaking with great pathos about Mrs. Bardell's revolting child, contains this reference:

> . . . and I shall prove to you, by a witness whose testimony it will be impossible for my learned friend to weaken or controvert, that on one occasion he patted the boy on the head, and after inquiring whether he had won any 'alley tors' or 'commoneys' lately (both of which I understand to be a particular species of marbles much prized by the youth of this town), made use of this remarkable expression: "How should you like to have another father?"

Piling on the agony, the Sergeant, in a later outburst, described the contrast in atmosphere: ". . . even the voice of the child is hushed; his infant sports are disregarded when his mother weeps; his 'alley tors' and his 'commoneys' are alike neglected; he forgets the long familiar cry of 'knuckle down' or at tip-cheese, or odd and even, his hand is out. . . ."

In the era of glass-ball stoppers lodged in the necks of mineral-water bottles, before the brass cap or clipped screwing cork ousted that novel corking process, children would extract the stoppers by cracking open the bottle-necks. This form of marble was termed "glasseys", a corruption of the happy simile, "glass-eye".

Gomme, in her *Traditional Games*, mentions the term "marididdles". These were likewise of amateur manufacture, made by the children themselves by rubbing and baking common clay.

For barter purpose, boys treated them as spurious. The stock-exchange scale for this form of barter had no violent percussions. The value was a constant. This was how it worked:

1 bary equals 4 stonies;
1 white alley equals 3 stonies.

Perhaps the most interesting aspect of marbles is its peculiar nomenclature. It is bizarre and eclectic in all the European languages wherein the game was—or is—played. "Bags fog" means "I claim first shot". Gomme used to have observers working up and down the country on her behalf, amateur reporters, but people interested in juvenile folklore, and she classified the material and information which they sent in. Some of the types of games recorded are: *Bridgeboard*, *Bun-hole*, *Cob*, *Hogo*, *Hoy Bang*, *Hundreds*, *Lag*, *Long Tawl*, *Nine Holes*, *Ring Taw*.

Of these, *Ring Taw* alone seems to have survived recent erosions. Only in the remotest parts of England does one meet a child whose mind leaps in recognition at the mention of the word "Taw". In out-of-the-way parts of Scotland and Ireland the game is still found, and there they have a still different jargon for the technicalities of the game. In Dublin, when marble-playing drew a peculiarly brief demand from my concentration, the King Marble was designated as "gull", while the nondescript hoi-polloi were known as "dabs".

To "shoot" or "fillip" (flip) a taw with precision is no easy task; the taw has to be placed upon the inside of the forefinger propelling it with the nail of the thumb. While a player is shooting his marble, his opponent can compel him to "knuckle down", in other words, to touch the ground with the middle joint of his forefinger. This is to ensure fair play (82).

84 The Game of Ring Taw

85 Bowling at Skittles

86 London Boys Playing Marbles

(*Photo Z. Glass*)

87 From an engraving by Jacob Cats, 1622, showing thirteen different games, of all seasons, including marbles

88 Dutch Children at Play
From *Houwelick, A Book of Emblems*, by Jacob Cats, *circa* 1642

Traditionally, the proper way to conserve and transport marbles was in a special bag, either in mesh form or hard-wearing fabric. My own playmates, however, seldom failed to find a trouser pocket equal to the task, and cloth bags among us would have suggested something rather effeminate, or have become an object for transient interest, like a curio.

Climate is obviously an important factor in determining the seasonal focus of play and makes it relative. The seasonable character of marble-playing was usually conveyed by a topical catch-phrase: "Marbles are out."

This unfailing slogan might often be interchanged with a similar one, "Buttons are out" (81), when, for the same cause that appoints inscrutably the time when a game shall succeed another, or for the reason of supply shortage or similar accident, marbles are out of favour.

In the days when buttons were numerous and paramount in juvenile attire, there was naturally a strong temptation for boys to cut them off their clothes and string them. Three types of button were known to the gamesters of not so long ago: (1) "Sinkeys", the metal buttons which had a slight hollow in the centre and holes for threading. On the market exchange a plain "sinkey" usually had the value of a unit, and was therefore called a "one-er". (2) Consisted of "shankeys", the variety that was attached by means of a shank, or loop of wire. Their value depended upon their size and beauty, ranging from "two-ers" to "three-ers". (3) "Liveries" were those lettered or heraldic buttons belonging to a livery servant, and the prize of all buttoners! "Sixers" existed, but were restricted to those large bronze buttons ornamented with foxes' heads and other devices, as worn by sportsmen.

The rules of conserving capital die hard and permeate widely. Buttons of a higher value were only kept as capital, since it was far more convenient to carry a dozen sixers on a string than seventy-two one-ers!

We can only reflect on whether this was a feature of the expansionist politico-economics of the era in which the practice evolved, or simply a function of that cycle of play-relations for which Nunn in his famous treatise on Play invented the name hormo-mnemic.

He meant that in our childhood we all pass through phases in play-patterns which are parallels for all the phases in the evolution of the human race, from primitivism and totem-worship to getting married and becoming independent! It remains to be seen whether this last-mentioned expedient was simply instinctive, or anticipatory of a chapter in human history still not closed.

October

Indoors once more, because of the wind and the rain, faces pressed against the window-pane of playroom or nursery, we look out at the dismal wintry days, tuning our minds to WINTER WEATHER SONGS and FIRESIDE GAMES with the climax, at the end of the month, of HALLOWE'EN.

Rain, rain, go away,
Come again another day,
Little Johnnie wants to play.

* * *

Rain, rain, go to Spain,
Never come back again!

THE NORTH WIND

The North Wind doth blow
And we shall have snow,
And what will Cock Robin do then, poor thing?
He'll sit in a barn
And keep himself warm
And hide his head under his wing, poor thing.

A WET DAY

Oh! the rain-clouds have covered the sky,
And the raindrops go dripping all day;
Not a bird flitting past can I spy,
How can little children be gay?

You could play us a tune full of glee
On your new little flute, Brother Phil.
If I play, will you dance? answered he,
Yes, Philip, says Kate, that I will.

* * *

Blow, wind, blow, and go, mill, go!
That the miller may grind his corn;
That the baker may take it, and into rolls make it,
And send us some hot in the morn.

* * *

In the game of *Tit-tat-toe*, which is played by very young boys with slate and pencil, this jingle is used:

Tit, tat, toe, my first go;
Three jolly butcher boys all in a row;
Stick one up, stick one down,
Stick one on the old man's crown.

Climate decides very often the kind of games children play in different countries. It is also responsible for some themes and subjects in their rhymes. Songs of blowing winds, and driving snow or rain, obviously belong to the countries experiencing a harsh winter. Our wind-toys, like kites and paper windmills, can be enjoyed in either March or December, but at our latitude no children brave the open air, quite naked, as do cherubs in the eighteenth-century French engraving (102).

* * * * *

TWO SCOTTISH HALLOWE'EN RHYMES

Hallowe'en ae nicht at e'en
I heard an unco squeekin;
Doleful Dumps has gotten a wife,
They ca' her Jenny Aiken.

Hey-how for Hallowe'en!
A the witches tae be seen,
Some black, and some green.
Hey-how for Hallowe'en.

In Ireland it is the custom "when young women would know if lovers are faithful" to put two nuts on the bars of the grate, naming the nuts after the lovers. If a nut cracks or jumps the lover will prove fickle, while if it begins to blaze or burn, he "has a regard for the person making the trial". But, if the nuts named after the girl and her lover burn together, it is a certain sign that they will be married. The Scottish custom was similar.

Then there is the celebrated spell in which an apple is eaten

89 Playing Snapdragon at a Hallowe'en Party
By Charles Keene

90 A Guessing Game
From an engraving of W. Holler

before a looking-glass with a view to discovering the inquirer's future husband who, it is believed, will be seen peeping over her shoulder. Some do this by candlelight.

Another unhallowed rite is to wet the sleeve of a shirt, hang it up by the fire to dry, and to lie in bed watching it till midnight, when the apparition of the individual's future partner for life will come in and turn the sleeve.

In Scotland, Hallowe'en is celebrated with haggis and mashed potatoes. In Wales, they would light bonfires (through which the young men would run, each casting a stone into the fire as they ran). Parsnips, nuts and apples were roasted in the ashes and in some places effigies were burnt.

WEXFORD: HALLOWE'EN CUSTOMS

The following is the verbatim account recorded from an octogenarian who spent her childhood in the Wexford area, about 1865–70:[1]

> First we prepared a great dish of colcannon. It was made during the day and kept until evening. It used to be made like this. First a layer of peeled potatoes were put in the pot, then a layer of parsnips and then a layer of white cabbage laid up fine—and then a layer of each again. A couple of leaves of cabbage and a quart of water and the pot would be stirring away till the lads came at night. Before the evening it would be pounded with a wooden pounder, and cream and butter added in plenty. Then the young fellows from all over the country around, would come, all dressed up, and if you didn't give them the colcannon—well, they might steal your plough, or take your gates off their hinges, lynch-pins off wheels, and any other damage they'd happen to think of. Afterwards there'd be great gaming like pouring melted lead into cold water and seeing what initial letter it would form into, this being the letter of your sweetheart, and games like Bob Apple and Forfeits. The boys would then go off around the parish still dressed-up on the look-out for more good things to eat.—(Recorded 12.4.41.)

HALLOWE'EN CUSTOMS (89)

When, in the second half of the eighteenth century, Rabie Burns wrote his poem "Hallowe'en", its observance was still

[1] Author's MS. collection.

general. A blazing fire, as might be expected, was an essential feature but so were nuts and apples.

In Scotland, to begin the proceedings, the boys and girls, blindfold and hand-in-hand, would go into the kailyard or kitchen garden, each pulling the first kailstock, or stock of colewort, which came to hand. Returning to the fireside, they would inspect their stalks, and, according as it was big or little, straight or crooked, so would the future wife or husband be, and the quantity of earth adhering would indicate the largeness or smallness of his or her fortune.

In these more sophisticated days girls and boys find no use for such superstitious practices; Hallowe'en, where it is still observed, is just another opportunity of harmless merry-making for the children.

Ducking for Apples on Hallowe'en

The Fireside Games of Hallowe'en are connected with ancient fire worship.[1] The Celtic Fire Festival of Beltane which took place on the first day of November celebrated the beginning of

[1] A. C. Haddon: Fire Games in *The Study of Man.*

winter. All private fires were put out. Only the "need", or sacrificial bonfire, was kindled amid ritual solemnity. From this, flame was taken on tapers, or kindling-wood, to the individual hearths.

Need-fire was made by nine men twisting a wimble of wood in a balk of oak until the friction made sparks fly. Dry agaric, a birch-tree fungus, was ignited with these and in turn brought to the private hearth. Like iron, need-fire was a defence against witches and devilry.

The Hallowe'en Party, to be fully "produced", demands decorations of fir branches and red-berried sprigs. A turnip is hollowed out, and a nose, eyes and mouth are cut to represent a human head. Then a lighted candle is placed inside and the turnip hung up as a grotesque presence presiding over the fun. Ghost stories are a traditional feature of the fireside, being so appropriate to All Souls' Night, and the mythology of the opening graves. But for children the most common and delightful game is *Bob Apple*.

A large tub is filled with water, and apples are placed on the bottom. The players each take a turn at grabbing an apple in their mouths. Hands may not be used, so that a ducking is the price paid for proving one's skill. Hence the uproarious laughter. Experienced "apple-bobbers" try for apples with longer stalks, which they nip between the teeth. But, since all the apples swirl and turn in the water, the difficulties are fairly shared.

During the Victorian period when this game was a household institution, a contemporary writer made this comment on the fashion:

> In recent years a practice has been introduced, probably by some tender mammas, timorous on the subject of their offspring catching cold, of dropping a fork from a height into the tub among the apples, and thus turning the sport into a display of marksmanship. It forms a very indifferent substitute for the joyous merriment of ducking and diving.
>
> But it very frequently happens that the candle comes round before they are aware and scorches them in the face or anoints them with grease. The disappointments and misadventures occasion, of course, abundant laughter.

For dry apple-bobbing, the fruit are hung from a tightly stretched cross-cord or clothes-line on separate vertical strings, and are secured by the mouth, hands being held behind the back.

GUESSING GAMES (90) FOR HALLOWE'EN REVELS

SEVEN RIDDLE-ME-REES[1]

Hoddy-doddy with a round black body,
Three legs and a wooden hat, what is that?

*   *   *

Hitty Pitty within the wall
Hitty Pitty without the wall;
If you touch Hitty Pitty,
Hitty Pitty will bite you.

*   *   *

Highty, tighty, paradighty, clothes in green,
The king could not read it, no more the queen,
They sent for a wise man out of the East,
Who said it had horns, but was not a beast.

[1] *Ree*, points out Crofton Croker, is a contraction of the old word *Reed*, meaning advice, knowledge, learning.

91 "Buck, buck, how many fingers have I got up?"

92 "How many fingers . . . ?"

93 Fourteenth century: *Roman d'Alexandre*

94 Sixteenth century: from a Dutch engraving

FORFEITS

Hick-a-more, Hack-a-more,
Hung on a kitchen door.
Nothing so long and nothing so strong
As Hick-a-more, Hack-a-more,
Hung on a kitchen door.

* * *

Lily-low, lily-low, set up on end,
See little baby go out at town end.

* * *

Little Nancy Etticoat with a white petticoat
And a red nose.
The longer she stands, the shorter she grows.

* * *

Flour of England, fruit of Spain,
Met together in a shower of rain,
Put in a bag, tied round with a string,
If you tell me this riddle I'll give you a ring.[1]

HUNT THE SLIPPER

This old-fashioned pastime is so universally known that it is scarcely necessary to describe it; however, as it forms one of the merriest indoor sports for long winter evenings, it would be a pity to omit it from this book (see p. 197).

Several boys seat themselves in a circle on the ground, and another, taking his place inside the ring, gives a slipper to one of them, by whom it is immediately and secretly handed to one of his neighbours; it is now passed round from one sitter to another with as much dexterity as possible, so as to completely perplex the "hunter" (or player standing in the middle) in his endeavours to "chase the slipper by its sound", and who must continue his search until successful; the player in whose possession it is found must in his turn "hunt the slipper", whilst the former hunter joins the sitters.

[1] (1) An iron pot; (2) a nettle; (3) a holly-tree; (4) a sunbeam; (5) a candle; (6) also a candle; (7) a plum-pudding.

FORFEITS

Incantation:

Here is a thing
A very pretty thing.
Pray tell us
What must the owner of this thing do?

Penalty:

(*Bow to the prettiest,*
Kneel to the wittiest
And kiss the maiden you love best.)

SOME FORFEIT GAMES FROM AN OLD PLAY-BOOK (94)

As a general rule, a game of forfeits is continued until each player has pledged three articles, but this arrangement may be modified according to circumstances.

THE FOUR ELEMENTS

The party being seated in a circle, the player who has been chosen to commence the game takes a knotted handkerchief, and throws it suddenly into another's lap, calling out at the same time either "Earth!" "Water!" "Air!" or "Fire!" If "Earth" be called out the player into whose lap the handkerchief has fallen must name some *quadruped* before the other can count ten; if "Water", he must name a *fish*; if "Air", a *bird*, and if "Fire", he must remain silent. Should the player name a wrong animal, or speak when he ought to be silent, he must pay a forfeit and take a turn at throwing the handkerchief; but should he perform his task properly he must throw the handkerchief back to the first player. Those who have never joined in this simple game can have no idea of the absurd errors into which the different players fall when summoned unawares to name a particular kind of animal.

THE FAMILY COACH

The chief player must possess the faculty of inventing a long story, as well as a tolerably good memory. This player gives to each of the others the name of some person or thing to be mentioned in the story he is about to relate. For example, he may call one "the coachman", another "the whip", another "the inn", another "the old gentleman", another "the footman", another "the luggage", and so on until he has named all the persons engaged in the game. The story-teller now takes his stand in the centre of the room and commences his narrative; in the course of which he takes care to mention all the names given to the players. When the name of a player is mentioned he must immediately rise from his seat, turn round and sit down again, or else pay a forfeit for his inattention, and whenever "the family coach" is named *all* the players must rise simultaneously. In the following example of a story the names given to the different players are printed in italics: "An *old gentleman* dreading an attack of the gout resolved to pay a visit to the hot wells of Bath; he therefore summoned his *coachman* and ordered him to prepare THE FAMILY COACH (all the players rise, turn and sit down again). The *coachman*, not liking the prospect of so long a journey, tried to persuade the *old gentleman* that THE FAMILY COACH was out of repair; that the *leader* was almost blind, and that he (the *coachman*) could not drive without a new *whip*. The *old gentleman* stormed and swore upon hearing these excuses and ordered the *coachman* out of the room, while the *little dog* sprang from under his master's chair and flew at the calves of the offender, who was forced to make a precipitate exit. Early the next morning THE FAMILY COACH belonging to the *old gentleman* stopped at an *inn* on the Bath road, much to the surprise of the *landlord*, who had never seen such a lumbering conveyance before. THE FAMILY COACH contained the *old gentleman*, the *old lady* (his wife) and the *little dog* that had made such a furious attack on the poor *coachman's* legs. The *landlord* called the *landlady*, who came bustling out of the *inn* to welcome the *old gentleman* and *old lady*. The *footman* jumped down from behind THE FAMILY COACH and helped the *old gentleman* and the *old lady* to alight, while the *boots* and *chambermaid* belonging to the *inn* busied themselves with the *luggage*. The *little dog* trotted after the *old lady*, but just as it was going into the *inn* the *coachman* gave it a cut with his *whip*. The *little dog* howled, upon which the *old gentleman* turned round, and, seeing the *coachman* with his *whip* raised, he seized him by the throat. The *footman* came to the assistance of his friend the *coachman*, and the *ostler* belonging to the *inn* took the side of the *old gentleman*. The *landlord*, *landlady*, *chambermaid*, *boots*, *cook*, *stable-boy*, *barmaid* and all the other inmates of the *inn* rushed into the road to see what was the matter, and their cries, joined to the yells of the *little dog* and the screams of the *old lady*, so frightened the *leader*, the *white horse* and the *brown mare* that they ran away with THE FAMILY COACH." This tale might have been continued to any length, but is sufficient to give the story-teller some idea of what is expected from him to keep up the fun of the game.

MY LADY'S TOILET

This game of forfeits is suited for a large party of boys and girls. Each player chooses the name of some article belonging to a lady's toilet, such as "mirror", "brush", "hairpin", "scent-bottle", and so on. One of the players then takes a wooden trencher, or any other circular object that is not liable to be broken, and twirls it round in the centre of the room, naming at the same time some toilet article, upon which the player who bears the name of such article starts from his seat and endeavours to catch the trencher before it falls, failing to do which he pays a forfeit and takes the spinner's place. The person who spins the trencher generally prefaces the name of the article with some such sentence as "My lady is going out for a walk and wants her *scent-bottle*". When the word "toilet" is called out by the trencher-spinner, all the players change their seats, and as the spinner takes care to secure a place one player necessarily finds himself without one, and has to pay a forfeit and twirl the trencher. If a player can catch the trencher before it falls he has no forfeit to pay, but he takes the spinner's place, just as though he had failed to accomplish this feat.

THE GAME OF THE KEY

This game may be played by any number of persons, who should all, except one, seat themselves on chairs placed in a circle, and he should take his station in the centre of the ring. All the sitters must next take hold, with their left hands, of the right wrists of the persons sitting on their left, being careful not to obstruct the grasp by holding the hands. When all have in this manner joined hands, they should begin moving them from left to right, making a circular motion and touching each other's hands, as if for the purpose of taking something from them. The player in the centre then presents a key to one of the sitters, and turns his back, so as to allow it to be privately passed to another, who hands it to a third, and so it is handed round the ring from one player to the other, with all imaginable celerity, which task is exceedingly easy to accomplish, on account of the continued motion of the hands of all the players. It is the office of the player in the centre, after allowing time for the key to be passed on to the third or fourth player, to watch its progress narrowly, and to endeavour to seize it in its passage. If he succeeds in his attempt, the person in whose hands it is found, after paying a forfeit, must take his place in the centre, and give and hunt the key in his turn; should the seeker fail to discover the key in his first attempt, he must continue his search until he succeeds. When a player has paid three forfeits, he is out.

ACTING RHYMES

The players being seated in a circle, one of them gives a simple word, to which each has to find a rhyme that can be expressed by some movement, grimace or inarticulate sound. Let us suppose that the first player proposes the word "bat"; the second player stands up and rubs his shoes on the carpet to signify that he is using a "mat"; the third player now commences to purr or mew like a "cat"; the fourth makes a low bow and raises an imaginary "hat" from his head; the fifth, if sufficiently active, scampers about the room on all fours like a "rat"; the sixth goes through certain antics supposed to pertain to a stage Irishman, by which he tries to intimate that he is "Pat"; and the first player, who is bound to find a rhyme for his own word, lies on his back and stretches out his hands so as to be perfectly "flat". If any player speaks while acting his rhyme, if he fails to make his actions intelligible, or if he cannot find a rhyme to the given word, he must pay a forfeit. The players take it by turns to propose a word, which should never consist of more than one syllable.

POST

This game is particularly adapted for a large party. One of the players, called "the postman", has his eyes bandaged as in *Blind Man's Buff* (95–99). Another volunteers to fill the office of "postmaster-general", and all the rest seat themselves round the room. At the commencement of the game the postmaster assigns to each player the name of a town, and if the players are numerous, he writes the names given to them on a slip of paper in case his memory should fail him. The postmaster-general retires to some corner whence he can overlook the other players. When he calls out the names of two towns, thus, "London to Halifax", the players who bear these names must immediately change seats, and as they run from one side of the room to another, the postman tries to capture them. If the postman can succeed in catching one of the players, or if he can manage to sit down on an empty chair, the player that is caught, or excluded from his place, becomes postman. The postmaster-general is not changed throughout the game unless he gets tired of his office. When a player remains seated after his name has been called, he must pay a forfeit, or, if the game is played without forfeits, he must go to the bottom of the class, which is represented by a particular chair, and to make room for him all the players who were formerly below him shift their places.

HOW? WHERE? AND WHEN?

One of the players is sent out of the room, while the others fix upon a subject which may be anything to which the three questions "How do you like it?", "Where do you like it?" and "When do you like it?" will apply. When the subject has been decided upon, the out-player is summoned. He now puts the first question to the nearest player, who returns him a puzzling answer; he then passes to the next, and repeats the same question; then to the next and so on until he has made the round of the room. If none of the answers enables him to guess the subject, he tries each player with the second question, and if the answers to this leave him still in the dark, he solicits a reply from each to the third and last question. Should the player fail to guess the subject after asking the three questions, he pays a forfeit and takes another turn outside, but should he succeed in guessing it during his rounds, the player last questioned must pay a forfeit and go out of the room in his place. The in-players should always endeavour to hit upon some word that has two or three meanings for a subject, as such a word renders the answers extremely confusing. For instance, if "Jack" be the subject decided on, one of the players may say in answer to the first query that he likes it "fried", referring to the fish called the Jack; in answer to the second that he likes it "before the kitchen fire", referring now to a roasting-jack; and in answer to the third, that he likes it when he is "dressing", now regarding the subject as a boot-jack.

CONCERT

The players, having selected a "conductor", seat themselves round him in a circle. The conductor now assigns to each a musical instrument, and shows how it is to be played. When all are provided with their imaginary instruments, the conductor orders them to tune, and by so doing, he gives each musician a capital opportunity for making all sorts of discordant noises. When the different instruments have been tuned, the conductor waves an unseen baton and commences humming a lively air in which he is accompanied by the whole of his band, each player endeavouring to imitate with his hands the different movements made in performing on a real instrument. Every now and then the conductor pretends to play on a certain instrument, and the player to whom it belongs must instantly alter his movements for those of the conductor, and continue to wield a baton until the chief player abandons his instrument. Should a player omit to take the conductor's office at the proper time, he must pay a forfeit. The fun of this game greatly depends on the humour of the conductor and the adroitness with which he relinquishes his baton and takes up the instruments of the other players.

GUESSING GAMES AND THE IRISH COUNTRYSIDE

One of the basic elements of traditional games, played in rural Ireland, especially in the Gaelic-speaking areas, seems to be a form of "sitting around in a circle". Nearly all the fireside amusements conform to this idea, so do a large number of the outdoor games played in the fields during the mowing or reaping seasons.

There is no more natural place or time for play than during the stooking of ripened corn in a sunlit field (100), or saving of the hay, or during the long bright evenings after the day's work has been rewarded with a welcome meal of cold tea, farmers' butter and griddle cake. Of all the games investigated, this "sitting around in a circle on the ground", with a leader, or master-player, to conduct the procedure, seems to be a predominant pattern in rustic play.

When it is recalled that such a large percentage of the Irish agrarian population have at one time or another been migratory workers in the bothies and harvest-fields of Scotland and England (more especially from the Irish-speaking areas in Donegal, Mayo and Sligo), it seems logical that an interchange of customs should have taken place on either side; yet we have no evidence that the Irish farm-workers *left* any lasting impression on the forms of English or Scottish rustic sports; on the other hand, that they *took away with them* ideas and traditional games, later to render them contributory to their own store of fun, and to colour them with a native idiom or with a localised phrase, seems very apparent. So many of these sitting-in-a-ring games involve tricky motions with hands or feet. A game, now

95 Fourteenth century: Hoodman Blind

96 Nineteenth century: Victorian children

97 Eighteenth century: Wood engraving

98 Thirteenth century

99 Eighteenth century: Drypoint

BLIND MAN'S BUFF

100 Country folk at a harvest festivity

101 After a Hayman painting in Vauxhall Gardens, 1862

BLIND MAN'S BUFF

obsolete but within this class, is one formerly known as *Johnny Hairy, Crap In*. Gomme[1] asserts that this is a variant of the English game *Hot Cockles*—a very ancient pastime indeed. It is a fireside game. All players sit round the fire and put out their right feet. Then the master of the game repeats this formula:

One-ery, two-ery, dickery, dary,
Wispy, spindy, smoke of the kindy,
Old Johnny Hairy, Crap In!

Each word is addressed to a man; when the leader comes to "Crap In!" the man specified draws in his foot. When all but one have drawn in their feet, that one must kneel down, and his eyes are blindfolded. The master of the game puts his elbow on his back, and strikes him with his elbow or fist, saying:

Hurley, burley, trump the trace,
The cow ran through the market-place,
Simon Alley hunt the buck,
How many horns stand up?

At the same time he holds up several fingers. The man kneeling down has to guess the number. If he guesses correctly, the master of the game takes his place. If he fails to guess, he is kept down and another man goes and strikes his back, and so on (92).

The above was a version recorded before 1890 in County Leitrim by Gomme's observer, a Mr. Duncan, who wrote concerning it as follows: "*Crap Isteach* is the Irish for 'Draw In', as in Flaherty's *Sports of Winter* there is a Gaelic version. This, I should imagine, makes it certain that, although well known elsewhere, the game also obtained in the West of Ireland."

Thus, in the above game, we observe a fusion of three distinct game-ideas: (*a*) the kneeling action, which is the basis of Ireland's *most* widespread sport, namely *Forfeits*; (*b*) the blindfolding idea, which is common to several of the *Blind Man's Buff* category; and (*c*) the guessing motif connected with the ancient Anglo-Norman form, *Buck, buck, how many horns do I hold up?* (91, 105), a guessing game of fingers deriving from the Roman formula *Bucca, bucca, quot sunt hic?* and mentioned by Petronius in his

[1] *Games*.

Satyricon. This traditional form takes another twist in a Ring Game entitled *Horns* or *The Painter*, introducing a comic theme of blackening the face, described in detail by Carleton in his prose sketch, *Larry MacFarland's Wake*:[1]

> A small fellow gets a lump of soot or lamp-black, and fixing a ring of boys and girls about him, he lays his two forefingers on his knees and says "Horns! Horns! Cow-horns!" Then, by a jerk, he raises his fingers above his head; the boys and the girls in the ring then do the same thing, for the meaning of the play is this: The man with the blackening *always* raises his fingers every time he names an animal; but if he names any that has *no* horns, and should the others jerk up their fingers then, they must get a stroke over the fingers with the soot. "Horns! Horns! Goat-horns!" then he ups with his fingers like lightning; they must all do the same, because a goat *has* horns. "Horns! Horns! Horse-horns!" He ups with them again, but the boys must not, because a horse has *not* horns. However, any one that raises them gets a slake. . . . It's a purty game . . . and maybe there's not fun in sticking the soot over the purty warm rosy cheeks of the colleens, while their eyes are dancing . . . och, och! . . .

HOT COCKLES (93)

One player with his eyes bandaged lays his head on a chair, or in another player's lap, while the others strike him on his back with their open hands. In this unenviable position he remains until he can guess who strikes him, when the striker takes his place. The poet Gay describes this pastime:

> *As at Hot Cockles once I laid me down,*
> *And felt the weighty hand of many a clown,*
> *Buxoma gave a gentle tap, and I*
> *Quick rose, and read soft mischief in her eye.*

This conception of a penalty being the principal cause of the fun, seems peculiar to the Gaelic temperament. Apart altogether from the theories of sadism at the root of primitive games, or the corrective principle effected through the medium of mockery for the loser, penalty games appear to outnumber all other forms of fireside (indoor), or harvesting (outdoor), amusement. Sometimes

[1] *Traits and Stories.*

it is a guessing game or a Riddle Rhyme or a variant of *Forfeits*, working up to the highlight of the sport, i.e. the moment when the unlucky loser suffers the kicks, knocks, pinches, or punches of his playmates. Sometimes the game is a fusion of two, or of all, of these forms. The task, penalty, or *trom* (onus, weight) idea is paramount. The Question-and-Answer jingles are frequent; and, in the Gaelic versions, a doggerel rhyme of *larabóg* is invariably the accompanying incantation.

THE GAME OF LURABÓG, LARABÓG[1]

The children of Connaught have a very curious game, according to Sean Mac Floinn of Tuam. They sit on the floor around the fire and they begin to say these words:

Lurabóg, larabóg,
Buide Ui Néill
Néill ag preaban
Preaban ag ruileach,

Suileac reicneac
Seicne meille
Ta cead loman
Loman lataige

ruirtan
bualtin
buille beag sa peicín
Crap isteach an fideóg (beilín, plaiceac)

Examples of these Indoor and Outdoor Ring Games, with a penalty or guessing principle running through them, may be sought and found in obscure Irish periodicals and other random sources.[2]

THE GAME OF CHURNS

A variety of *Forfeits*, with a *House-that-Jack-Built* formula inside a four-form pattern.

It should be stressed that in these Penalty Games the comic element is related to the impulse to *humiliate*, and not to the unconscious sadism that marks, say, the bird-catching custom of the Wren Boys. Thus, in the kissing penalty exerted in the game of *Weds or Forfeits*, discussed in the next section, the incongruity begets laughter. And in laughter, writes Bergson, "we always

[1] O'Flaherty, *Siamsa an Geimridh*, Dublin (1892).
[2] *An Stoc*, vol. II, (1924), Munster Gaeltacht.

find an unavowed attention to HUMILIATE, and consequently to CORRECT our neighbour, if not in his will, at least in his deed."

The different patterns take their names from farming epithets, *Churns*, *Selling Oats*, *Sacks*, a nomenclature that derives from an imagery that is essentially local, in common with the Penalty Games played by Provençal, Basque and Spanish children.

THE GAME OF TROM, TROM, CAD TÁ ÓS DO CIONN?[1]

Whoever speaks or laughs
Until this time tomorrow
He'll get twenty slaps,
Twenty knocks,
Twenty bites of an ant,
And twenty kicks of a horse.

Each player recites one line of this doggerel, and the child on whom the last line falls, draws in his boot. The process is repeated till all feet are withdrawn, except the last unfortunate one. The leader stands over him, places his right elbow on the victim's back, and knocks his elbow alternately thereon, and on the palm of his own hand, saying as he does so:

Cnugaide, cnagaide
i lap do droma-ra
isteach bpoll as airce
Cia mnéid adharc air an bpocán poic?
(*Knick knack, the small of your back,*
into a hole, out of a hole,
How many horns has the buck goat?)

which in practice means, "How many fingers have I got up?" If he guesses right, he is released, but if he fails they place a heavy object on his back, crying:

Trom, trom, etc. . . .
(*Heavy, heavy on your back,*
What doesn't concern you . . . leave it be!)

The game then takes the form of *Forfeits*.

O'Flaherty shows other variants as occurring in places in County Tyrone (p. 78), County Armagh (p. 79, II) and Barnac (County Galway). On p. 18 he cites examples from Connemara and County Meath. Whereas an English variant is also given:

[1] *Irisleabhar na Gaedhilige*, vol. XIII, p. 315.

Mrs. Fitzhenry, I invite you to dinner,
To eat a piece of roasted frog,
Come all you good people,
Look over the steeple,
To see the cat play with the dog.
Larum larum, lumber, lock,
Five miles, seven o'clock,
Wessat, we sung,
Till daylight sprung
Till little Tom came in
With his long rod
And tipped us all
From wig to wag
With my biggeldy, pickeldy pie.

This is a remarkable nonsense-sequence with rhythmic values and imagery comparable to the best verses in the Lewis Carrol manner. How did it evolve in an Irish area? In all likelihood from a (now obsolete) English nursery rhyme, a metrical line which preserves the trochaic beat that we have alluded to in an earlier chapter:

Intery, mintery, cutery, corn,
Apple seed and apple thorn,
Wine, briar, limber-lock,
Five geese in a flock.

Other variants of the *Lurabóg* game, one with a "blindfolded-cum-forfeits" motif, the other with a dramatic enactment of a judge on the bench, occur in the Gaelic periodical *An Cearnóg*, and are described in similar detail by Pilib O Caldraite.

Other variants of *Ceann an Staca* occur in *An Locrann*[1] in a contribution from Sean O Catasaig, variant No. 3 of which is played to a different rhyme:

What might you be eating?
  Bread and cake.
Where is my share of it?
  The white cat ate it.
Where is the white cat?
  Under the sticks . . . etc.

Forfeits in County Donegal is known as the *Game of Contraries*,

[1] Christmas 1911, p. 3, col. 1.

while in Cork it has been observed to be the culmination point in a game like *Drop Handkerchief*, having the opening formula:

I wrote a letter to my love
And on the way I dropped it,
It wasn't you, it wasn't you, it was YOU!

Thus, whether the incantation be "Lurabóg", "Intery-mintery", or "I wrote a letter", the pattern of *Forfeits* is always the same. The article pledged is always held up by the crier, above the head of the kneeling child, *who must not see it*. The invocation goes:

I've got a thing, a very pretty thing,
What has the owner of this pretty thing to do?

It recalls the invocation to some oracular power, analogous to the game of counting petals in order to foretell the name of a sweetheart (i.e. "He loves me, he loves me not", etc.), or "Mirror, mirror, tell me true", etc., both being of unmistakably pre-Christian origins (see p. 115, No. 1).

In the West of Ireland, to this day, the custom of smacking as a form of penalty (*trom*) is still the most mirth-raising sport.

This curious tradition of kicking, beating, bumping, or tapping of noses has a precedent in games of the Middle Ages. Thus, in Rabelais[1] we find a reference to *Croquinolles*, which is the name for a sport in which taps on the nose form the basis of the enjoyment. Other variants were *Croquinole* and *Chiquenaude*. A fifteenth-century reference in *La Mystère de Saint Quentin*[2] contains the lines:

Pour rompre testes et canoles
pour leur donner des croquignoles.

It may be that this form of amusement derived from an impulse to caricature the knights who entered the lists to do battle with lance and spear and much jostling for position. A further mention by Rabelais describes the game *Pimpompet*, one in which the players kick each other on the behind. The name, in all probability, translates the sound of the kicks given. Compare the modern French *pompon*.

[1] *Gargantua*, vol. II, chap. 7. [2] Line 4326.

This form of knocking together of bottoms has an offshoot in a nameless game quoted in the Gaelic magazine *Lúgnasa*:[1] "Two children put their backs to one another and then link arms and each, in turn, lifts the other from off the ground on to his back, meanwhile saying the following:

Mead mead cáise
Mead mead ím
Mead mead an buacaillín
Síos go dtí na buinn."

A curious phenomenon in examining these rhymes in Gaelic is that an element of bilingualism frequently occurs, having the aural effect of a highly sophisticated doggerel verse:

Meig-eg ar san gabhar
What's that arsan caora
Bedad arsan gabar
Tá béarla ar an gcaora.

Madam indirde (the woman is in the
upper window of a house?)
Would you buy a bardal?
Is he fat?
Go deimhin nu cat
Acht laca beag breac
A deanfad duit leas
Is bhi se mar peata ag mo mamai.

Yesterday morning maidininde
I killed a goose Maire me gé
The knife was too sharp bi an sgian
ró géar
I cut my finger gearr mé mo mhéar.

Méadg Méadg
Mil ar méis
Luct an arbair
'Gam a marbuigan
Raoìn gráinìn arbair
dir me areir
Méadg Méadg
Méadg Méadg

Nì truimad an loc an laca
Nì truimide an eac a scrian
Nì truimide an caora a collain
Agus nì truimide an calainn ciall.[2]

[1] 1923, p. 2, col. 1.

[2] P. Ó. Caldraite.

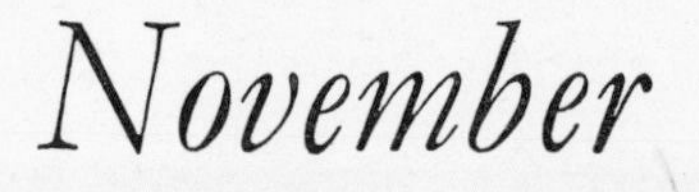

November

This month, half-way between autumn's cornucopia and the climacteric of Christmastide, is the season, more than others, of the indoor party games. Because the days are short and dismal, the Children's Party fits well into November's sequence—and welcome particularly is the child who has a birthday now, for the guests who are invited can enjoy the brightly lit and decorated

102 Playing with Paper Windmills

103 A Ring Game
Seventeenth century

104 Hunt the Slipper, 1804

105 "How many fingers have I got up?"
From a Victorian picture-book

room and play the same popular traditional games which our grandparents played(103), such as: HUNT THE SLIPPER(104), POSTMAN'S KNOCK and MUSICAL CHAIRS.

MUSICAL CHAIRS[1]

Universally popular as an indoor game. Dr. Jamieson points out that in Scotland the game is known as *Change Seats, the King's Coming*, and is played as this in Lothian and the south of Scotland.

According to him it is supposed to ridicule the political scramble for places on the occasion of a change of government.

[1] These four tunes are suitable for Musical Chairs.

17

THE MILL WHEEL

Musical games are always enjoyed. One of the oldest and prettiest of indoor musical games is the *Mill Wheel*.

Each boy chooses a girl-partner, and the couples arrange themselves in a large ring—boys inside, girls outside. If there are not enough boys, girls may take their place, a ribbon or handkerchief being tied on one arm to distinguish them.

One boy is left over, and plays the part of Miller. He stands inside the ring, and the wheel begins to turn; in other words, the couples begin to march round, arm in arm, singing the following jingle:

There was a jolly miller
And he lived by himself
As the wheel went round
He made his wealth.

One hand on the hopper
And another in the bag;
As the wheel went round
He made his grab.

At the word "grab" all the boys move forward one place, and the Miller tries to secure a partner. If he succeeds, then the boy left out becomes the Miller. If not, the first Miller keeps his place, and once more the wheel begins to turn.

Each time, at the word "grab", the same change of partners takes place.

Sometimes, as a variety, the couples face about, and thus the wheel must turn in the opposite direction. If this change be made suddenly by the leading couple, it causes a moment of merry confusion before the wheel turns smoothly. A further variation is for the girls to march inside and the boys outside—in which case, of course, there would be a girl Miller.

PUSS IN FOUR CORNERS

Four players take their stations in the four corners of a room, and a fifth called "Puss" places himself in the middle of it; the players in the corners then change places by running to the opposite ends, and Puss must endeavour to get into one of the vacant places before the opposite player is able to reach it; if he can do so, the player thus out becomes Puss.

Popular throughout all rural Ireland, in parts of Wexford it was called *Fillie Four Corners* (a corruption of *Phil i' Four Corners*?).

GAMES OF THE QUIET LIFE

Watching Pictures in the Firelight is an Adventure too.

THE GUNPOWDER PLOT (106)

Give me a penny, do, dear Aunt,
Louisa said one day;
And do not ask me what I want,
But give it to me, pray!

106 "Please to remember the fifth of November . . ."
From a print of 1821

107 Singing Carols
By Phiz (Hablot K. Browne)

108 Clearing the snow and bringing in the holly

MUMMER RHYMES

O Christmas is coming
The geese are getting fat,
Won't you please put a penny
In a poor man's hat.
If you haven't got a penny
A ha'penny will do.
If you haven't got a ha'penny
Then God bless you!

AN OLD TYME GREETING

Ha wish ye a merry Christmas
An' a Happy New Year
A pantry full a' good roast beef
An' a barril full a' beer.

In the full year's almanac of games and gladness, it is Christmastide when childhood's annual miracle takes place. The vision of Santa Claus breathlessly waited for: the thought of his coming, whether in his Continental rôle of benign Saint Nicholas, or as the red-robed, white-bearded jolly patriarch who rides on reindeer-drawn sledge above the roofs, to the jingle of sleigh-bells nobody ever hears, excites and obsesses the child-consciousness. Each day is impatiently counted.

Then, somehow, all the magic and lore of time-old family tradition are summed up for the festival of peace and goodwill and good cheer. The cutting and hanging of holly (108) sets the key for all the pageantry and party spirit that go with what has become to be known as "A White Christmas". The hanging of the mistletoe, its Druidic associations quite forgotten, means that Father Christmas is well set on his course from the Polar North and due to land very soon indeed.

The spangled tree, the candles and crackers and cake, the waits and the singing of carols (107), the dressing up—mummer-like—for the school play, Nativity or Morality, the longed-for visits to pantomime, circus, toy bazaar gratified—all are overshadowed by the reality of the brimming sack.

Its bounty of toys, asked for, prayed for, and passionately expected, yet each one a surprise, crowns the season when, first thought on waking, the stocking's owner runs to the chimney-piece or the bed-rail to seek and find his heart's desire.

The custom of the Christmas-tree was brought to England from the Continent, when Queen Victoria introduced it into her household (109). After that it was popularised rapidly and has since come to be regarded as part of the British Christmas tradition.

CUSTOMS ON CHRISTMAS EVE[1]

There is a Christmas custom here which pleased and interested me. The children make little presents to their parents, and to each other, and the parents to their children. For three or four months before Christmas the girls are all busy, and the boys save up their pocket-money to buy these presents. What the present is to be is cautiously kept secret; and the girls have a world of contrivances to conceal it—

[1] A letter written by Coleridge to his "Friend" while travelling in northern Europe.

109 Christmas-tree, lucky dip and distribution of presents

110 "The Raptures of the Very Little Ones"
After a painting by Jan Steen (1626–79)

such as working when they are out on visits, and the others are not with them, getting up in the morning before daylight, etc. Then on the evening before Christmas Day, one of the parlours is lighted up by the children, into which the parents must not go; a great yew bough is fastened on the table at a little distance from the wall, a multitude of little tapers are fixed in the bough, but not so as to burn it till they are nearly consumed, and coloured paper, etc., hangs and flutters from the twigs. Under this bough the children lay out in great order the presents they mean for their parents, still concealing in their pockets what they intend for each other. Then the parents are introduced, and each presents his little gift; they then bring out the remainder one by one from their pockets, and present them with kisses and embraces. Where I witnessed this scene there were eight or nine children, and the eldest daughter and the mother wept aloud for joy and tenderness; and the tears ran down the face of the father, and he clasped all his children so tight to his breast, it seemed as if he did it to stifle the sob that was rising within it. I was very much affected. The shadow of the bough and its appendages on the wall, and arching over on the ceiling, made a pretty picture; and then the raptures of the very little ones, when at last the twigs and their needles began to take fire and snap—O it was a delight to them! On the next day (Christmas Day) in the great parlour, the parents lay out on the table the presents for the children (110); a scene of more sober joy succeeds; as on this day, after an old custom, the mother says privately to each of her daughters, and the father to his sons, that which he has observed most praiseworthy and that which was most faulty in their conduct. Formerly, and still in all the smaller towns and villages throughout these parts, the presents were sent by all the parents to some one fellow, who in high buskins, a white robe, a mask and an enormous flax wig, personates Knecht Rupert, i.e. the servant Rupert. On Christmas night he goes round to every house, and says that Jesus Christ, his Master, sent him thither. The parents and elder children receive him with great pomp and reverence, while the little ones are most terribly frightened. He then inquires for the children, and, according to their character which he hears from the parents, he gives them the intended present (111), as if they came out of heaven from Jesus Christ. Or, if they should have been bad children, he gives the parents a rod, and, in the name of his Master, recommends them to use it frequently. About seven or eight years old, the children are let into the secret and it is curious how faithfully they keep it (112).—S. T. Coleridge.

The first day of Christmas my true love sent to me
A partridge in a pear-tree.
The second day of Christmas my true love sent to me
Two turtle-doves and a partridge in a pear-tree.
The third day of Christmas, my true love sent to me
Three French hens and two turtle-doves and a partridge in a pear-tree.
The fourth day of Christmas my true love sent to me
Four colly birds, three French hens, two turtle-doves and a partridge in a pear-tree.
The fifth day of Christmas, my true love sent to me
Five gold rings, four colly birds, three French hens,
Two turtle-doves, and a partridge in a pear tree.
The sixth day of Christmas, my true love sent to me
Six geese a-laying, five gold rings, four colly birds,
Three French hens, two turtle-doves and a partridge in a pear-tree.
The seventh day of Christmas my true love sent to me
Seven swans a-swimming, six geese a-laying, five gold rings,
Four colly birds, three French hens, two turtle-doves and a partridge in a pear-tree.
The eighth day of Christmas my true love sent to me
Eight maids a-milking, seven swans a-swimming, six geese a-laying,
Five gold rings, four colly birds, three French hens, two turtle-doves and a partridge in a pear-tree.

The ninth day of Christmas my true love sent to me
Nine drummers drumming, eight maids a-milking, seven swans
A-swimming, six geese a-laying, five gold rings, four colly
Birds, three French hens, two turtle-doves and a partridge in a pear-tree.
The tenth day of Christmas my true love sent to me
Ten pipers playing, nine drummers drumming, eight maids a-milking,
Seven swans a-swimming, six geese a-laying, five gold rings,
Four colly birds, three French hens, two turtle-doves and a partridge in a pear-tree.
The eleventh day of Christmas my true love sent to me
Eleven ladies dancing, ten pipers playing, nine drummers drumming,
Eight maids a-milking, seven swans a-swimming, six geese a-laying,
Five gold rings, four colly birds, three French hens, two turtle-doves and a partridge in a pear-tree.
The twelfth day of Christmas my true love sent to me
Twelve lords a-leaping, eleven ladies dancing, ten pipers playing,
Nine drummers drumming, eight maids a-milking,
Seven swans a-swimming, eight geese a-laying, five gold rings,
Four colly birds, three French hens, two turtle-doves and a partridge in a pear-tree.

Traditionally, *Twelve Days* was played every Twelfth Night. It began as a sort of tongue-twister game, like *My Lady's Lap Dog* or *Twelve Huntsmen with Horns and Hounds*. And, judging from the old records, it ended as a Game of Forfeits arising out of the mistakes people make in trying to pronounce a string of alliterative nonsense like this:

Eight flip flap floating fly boats
Seven swans a-swimming
Six bottles of Frontignac
Five Limerick oysters
Four Persian cherry-trees
Three grey elephants
Two plumed partridges and
My Lady's Lap Dog.

In another form, more vulgarised, it enjoys the name of *The Gaping Wide-mouthed Waddling Frog*,[1] in which the words are purposely chosen to tongue-trip the speaker.

For such as these games, people sat in a circle. Grown-ups within the family circle used to join with the excited children, whose eyes and thoughts were only just kept off the mince-pies and the table spread for the feast that followed.

[1] *Vide* Halliwell's *Nursery Rhymes* (1842), p. 246.

Then each person in succession used to repeat the gifts of the day that raised his fingers to correspond with the number mentioned. The game has parallels in French and Spanish, and the grandiose or luxurious images feature in them also. The continuity of the rigmarole places it in the same class as those ancient songs known as *The Chants of Numbers* (like "One Old Oxford Ox Opening Oysters", or "One Man Went to Mow . . . a Meadow") and *The Chants of the Creed* (like "Who Knoweth One . . . I Knoweth One") of which versions can be traced back to Hebrew, Christian and Druidic origins.

* * * * *

The Scots call it *The Yule Days*, but they went on to thirteen verses, maybe in a spirit of counter-superstition. Here is the last round of the song as sung in Scotland:

The King sent his Lady on the thirteenth Yule day,
Three stalks o' merry corn, three maids a-merry dancing,
Three hinds a-merry hunting, an Arabian baboon,
Three swans a-merry swimming,
Three ducks a-merry laying, a bull that was brown,
Three goldspinks, three starlings, a goose that was grey,
Three plovers, three partridges, a papingo-aye;
Wha learns my carol and carries it away?

ST. STEPHEN'S DAY CUSTOMS

Country children in humble circumstances love dressing up because old custom entitles them to earn in this way, upon recognised days, the few pennies that go to the sweet-shop or the village toy-shop.

Thus red-letter days in their year are May Day, All Saints' Eve (Hallowe'en) and Saint Stephen's Day. These three dates, as Bett points out, were the occasion of the principal fire festivals among the ancient Celtic peoples.

Hence, in Scotland, Wales, Ireland and the Isle of Man has survived longer than elsewhere (and in Ireland still is followed) a custom known as *Wren Boys*. The earthenware or clay box with a slit in it, in which apprentices carried the wren through the streets on the Feast of St. Stephen, was known as the Christmas Box; in the Isle of Man, the Wren Box; hence the popular name of Boxing Day.

111 "Look what Santa Claus has brought me . . ."

112 Most utterly absorbed!

113 *Time, like a morning hoop, will roll from Christmastide to New Year's Day . . . .*

114 *And guide to its appointed goal the cyclic pageantry of play*

Journeying through town or village, dressed in old clothes borrowed from their elders, and strolling along in talkative gangs like fantastic mummers in miniature, tradition permits these children to invade gardens and private grounds, and to invite (and expect!) gifts of real currency in return for the chanting of the rhyme and the exhibition of the live wren that the drama demands.

If the Robin Redbreast has been elected by legend as the children's favourite, the tiny wren is the victim of myth. He enjoys a more hostile publicity than does the meek and friendly robin who, folklore asserts, tried to pull out with his beak the nails from the Saviour's hands—and wears a scarlet stigma as a reward for his charity. *He* merely outwitted the eagle. Flying, concealed in the feathers of the giant's back, he rose nearer to the seat of the gods, and claims leadership as a reward for his enterprise. Folklore has allowed him this. The wren is the apotheosis of ingenuity—some would say cunning—winning over brute force. And so, by brute force, he is mercilessly pursued, overpowered and sacrificed by a folk ritual older than the dark snakes of a D. H. Lawrence prose poem.

Yet in old nursery books the robin and the wren are linked. Says a jingle of 1829:

The Robin Redbreast and the Wren
Are God's cock and hen.

The lads who religiously carry out the ritual each year are not of the well-to-do section of the community. They are country youngsters who like dressing up and a legitimate excuse for invading the lands of the comfortable and for collecting whatever generosity bestows.

Up with your kettle, down with your pan,
A penny or tuppence to bury the rann.

Obviously there are regional variants, and like the mummer-play texts, new fragments and distortions and localisms have been introduced.

The *tum-ti-tum* jingle has a parallel in the Gaelic version, a factor unique in children's Singing Games. In rhythm, sentiment and in its mercenary motive it resembles the English equivalent:

A dreolín, a dreolín,
A riogh na n-éan,
Is mór í do mhuirgín
Is beag tú féin
Éirighsuas a bhean a' tighe
Agus tabhair duinn ubh
Na circe duibhe
A tá sa nid, ar chúl a tighe.

A free translation would be:

The wren, the wren,
King of the Birds,
Her pride is great
Though herself be tiny
Rise up O woman of the house
And give us an egg from the black hen
That's in the nest
At the back of the house.

If the untutored children of the Gaeltacht regard a fresh egg as the apex of their desires, in contrast to the rising generation of bilingual cynics to whom even the prospect of hard cash would not make old custom attractive, perhaps we in egg-rationed Britain appreciate their point.

Hunting the Wren is followed in Scotland also. In the Isle of Man the wren was still hunted up to the middle of the last century. It was carried by boys from door to door and suspended by the legs in the centre of two hoops. These crossed each other at right angles and were decorated with evergreen and ribbons. In return for a coin, earned by the chant, they gave a feather of the wren, so that before the end of the day the wren hung featherless. A superstitious value was attached to these feathers, for the possession of one of them was among sailors considered an effective charm against shipwreck during the coming year. At this time the bird was not buried in the churchyard (as in the Breton custom), but on the lonely sea-shore. In Ireland, once the Wren Boys have had their fun, the tiny creature is liberated from its wicker basket or home-made cage unhurt.

The reference to "kettles and pans" (p. 210) offers a link with a Welsh set of verses that celebrates the cutting-up[1] of the bird with "hatchets and cleavers" in preference to "knives and forks";

[1] cf. French song *L'Alouette*.

the boiling in "cauldrons and pans" instead of kettles and pots; and its conveyance in a "waggon or cart" instead of on "four men's shoulders".

This, in turn, points to an obvious link with the *Cutty Wren*, an ancient traditional English part-song which has received wider notice through its inclusion in Workers' Musical Association concerts, pageants and a gramophone recording. In this song the representative huntsmen in English are Robbin, Bobbin, Richard and John-all-alone. In Scotland, these same prototypes become Fozie-Mozie and Johnny Rednosie and Foslin, in addition to "brethren and kin". In Wales, their opposite numbers are Milder, Malder, Festel, Fose and John the Rednose.

A. L. Lloyd, in his study of ballads, *The Singing Englishman*, saw more than the tenacious survival of a pagan sacrificial ceremony in the words of this song. He associates the cryptic verses about sharp instruments with political conspiracy and the dialogue between Milder and Malder with secret societies of desperate men, outlawed by the Church as celebrants at witches' sabbaths and agitating against the barons. "Before the fourteenth century," says Lloyd, "the tyrant wren had become a symbol for baronial property."

Such politico-social postscripts to the work of folklorists like Frazer and Halliwell must command our attention. But the tentacles of tradition, with their claws of magic, time-old rite and folk-custom, cling fast and should not be overlooked. There is more than meets the ear in such a nursery shred as:

Robbin-a-Bobbin bent his bow
Shot at a woodcock and killed a yowe.
The yowe cried ba and ran away
And never came back till Midsummer day.

* * * * *

Bird weddings are common themes in children's folklore. A toy-book of 1744 contains *The Courtship of Cock Robin and Jenny Wren* and attributes the hero's death to the carelessness of the sparrow.

In remote pockets of rural life the ceremonials of wren-chasing still resist the spread of modern sophistication. Once the heritage of mediæval peasants, such shreds of pagan custom have become meaningless formulæ handed down from children to children—the true guardians of folk-literature nowadays.

Usually the preservation is the work of country children raised in villages, hamlets and isolated backwaters in the British Isles, offspring of humble people who passed on the ancient riddles, chants and folk-rhymes. They die hard, these folk-customs; they are dying slowly. But dying out, they surely are.

To this day, in rural Ireland, children still keep up a very old practice connected with Sacrificial Hunting. It is called *Hunting the Wren*, and takes place on St. Stephen's Day. In France the wren used to be hunted on Christmas Eve and given to the priest, who realised it in the church.

THE WREN-BOYS' RHYME

An Irish Mummer Custom

The rann, the rann, the King of all birds,
St. Stephen's Day she was caught in the furze,
Though she is little, her family's great,
O Luck for me lady, and give us a treat.

Me boots is worn, me clothes is torn,
Following the rann three miles or more,
So up with the kettle and down with the pan,
Give us an answer before we go on,
Put your hand in your pocket,
From that to your purse,
If ye don't give us money, we'll give ye our curse,
If ye don't give us money, if ye don't give us mate (*i.e. meat*)
We'll bury the rann at the pier of the gate,
Up with your kettle, down with your pan,
A penny or tuppence to bury the rann.

There is the myth of the winter solstice and the intertwining Christian belief of the Twelve Days. Thus, J. G. Frazer[1] makes the point that the custom of killing the divine animal stands in no relation to agriculture. It belongs to an early stage of social evolution, possibly before man tilled the land. The animal that was slaughtered, he shows, was generally looked upon as the

[1] *Golden Bough* (1902), vol. II, p. 442.

representative of a certain clan. Small birds were sacrificially hunted all over western Europe.

The inference is, therefore, paradoxically, that the scapegoat can be a bird. If so, then the practice of slaying the wren may represent the custom of killing the king "of the woods" at a later stage of social development. Else why should we have a universal folklore pattern of the wren-king, instead of just a custom restricted to English (i.e. local) history? For the primitive urge to sacrifice a real king dates back far into our past; and we should remember that in Greek the wren was *basiliskos* and in Latin *rex avium*; in France he is *roitelet*, in Italy *reatino*; in Spanish they call him *reyezuelo*, and in German *Zaunkönig*. In Wales he is *bren*—a Celtic ancestor of *vren*, and so we come to *wren*.[1]

The Wren Boys, though they know it not, scampering along lanes and footpaths on St. Stephen's Day, are the last custodians of a very pagan notion, taken over by the early Church. The 27th of December was the beginning of the New Year, according to the old reckoning. And these bands of innocents are simply dramatising the widespread pagan belief that the creature which was slain during the winter solstice, at its close starts a new lease of life.

* * * * *

A CHRISTMAS RING SONG

Here we go round the mulberry-bush,
The mulberry-bush, the mulberry-bush,
Here we go round the mulberry-bush
On Christmas Day in the morning.

* * * * *

The Christmas season brings toys and amusements to all children, and it does not take many moments before they congregate out of doors and show off what they have been given by fond friends and relations.

Soon the novelty of "newness" wears off, and the call of the open spaces turns their attention to old-time toys.

[1] Lina Eckenstein, *Comparative Studies* (1906), p. 172.

For the gusty day and the open spaces there is the exhilaration of flying kites, but for milder days and unmuddied ways, there is always the thrill of trundling hoops (113, 114).

FLYING KITES

Fly your kite on Monday
'Twill sail away so high.
Fly your kite on Tuesday
It will not reach the sky.
Fly your kite on Wednesday
It may go to the moon.
Fly your kite on Thursday
It won't come down till noon.
Fly your kite on Friday
'Twill try to reach the sun.
Fly your kite on Saturday
And then the week is done.
Fly, fly, ever so high!
How I should like to go up to the sky.
But I'd rather fly like a bird on the wing
Than fly like a kite that is tied to a string.

Mr. Nahum seems to have liked best those (rhymes) that make a picture, or sound racy, gay and sweet and so carry the fancy away. Any little fytte or jingle or jargon of words that manages *that* is like a charm or a talisman, and to make new ones is as hard as to spin silk out of straw, or to turn beech leaves into fairy money. When one thinks too of the myriad young voices that generation after

generation have carolled these rhymes into the evening air, and now are still—well, it's a thought no less sorrowful for being strange, and no less strange for the fact that our own voices too will some day be silent.

WALTER DE LA MARE in *Come Hither.*[1]

F for Francis
I for Iancis
N for Nickley Boney
I for Iohn the Waterman
and S for Signey Coney.

[1] "About and Roundabout", 1941.

INDEX

Numerical references in bold face are to fig. numbers of photographic illustrations; references in italic are to illustrations in the text; references in ordinary type are to text proper.